Gen. W.C. Lee

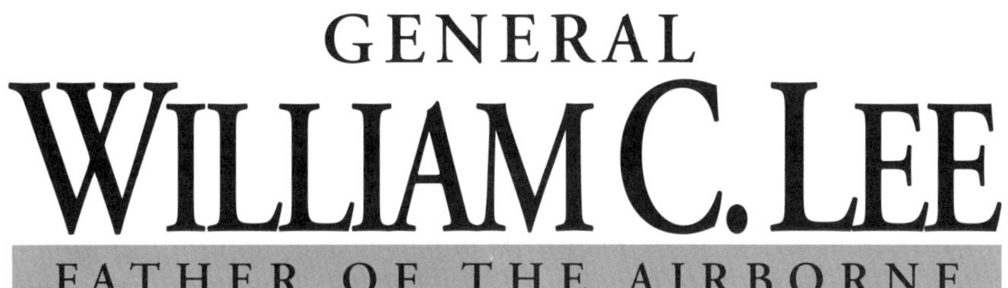

Just Plain Bill

GENERAL WILLIAM C. LEE

FATHER OF THE AIRBORNE

Just Plain Bill

by

Jerry Autry

assisted by Kathryn Autry

AIRBORNE PRESS

SAN FRANCISCO • RALEIGH

All photographs, letters and speeches came from the personal archives of General Lee and Mrs. Dava Lee, held in trust by Mrs. Lee's nephew, Harry Driver and used with his permission. Over the course of General Lee's life, he was given hundreds of photos; some were credited but most were not. We would especially like to credit the U. S. Army Military History Department, 82nd Airborne Division Memorial Museum; the Don F. Platt Museum at Fort Campbell, Kentucky; the *Daily Record*; the *Raleigh News and Observer*; *Time* magazine; and various other publications saved by General and Mrs. Lee whose origin could not be determined.

Cover and book design by Sue Knopf.

LIBRARY OF CONGRESS CATALOGING-IN-PUBLICATION DATA
General William C. Lee: father of the airborne/edited and compiled by Jerry Autry, assisted by Kathryn Autry.
p. cm.
Includes bibliographical references.
ISBN 0-934145-24-5
1. Lee, William C.
2. Generals-United States-Biography.
3. United States. Army. Airborne Division, 101st-History-sources.
I. Autry, Jerry, 1939- . II. Autry, Kathryn, 1960-.
U53.L397G46 1995
355'.0092-dc20
[B] 95-8104
CIP

First Edition, 1995
00 99 98 97 96 95 10 9 8 7 6 5 4 3 2

Printed in the United States of America

Airborne Press
3009 Dorner Circle
Suite C
Raleigh, N. C. 27606

Dedicated to all the

citizens of Dunn, North Carolina

(Best little town under the sun.)

This is a dedication that would please General Lee.

Acknowledgments

One of my favorite Biblical scenes is the one where God tolerated the constant failures of David because David always had such a thankful heart. I often feel this way—so incredibly thankful.

Acknowledgments are usually where those folks who contributed immeasurably to the making of a book are mentioned. To do true justice to them would be impossible, but I have to try. Of course, to leave someone out is inexcusable; and, if that happens, on subsequent reprints, those oversights will be remedied.

Thanks to Hoover Adams for his friendship all these years and for involving me in the General Lee celebration from the very beginning. When I first began to think of writing about General Lee, I wrote Hoover and asked him what he thought. When I visited Dunn through the years, Hoover always made time for me. There's no other individual I know who loves his country, the military, and General Lee more. As I've gone through General Lee's papers , the personal affection he had for Hoover is very evident. It's obvious to all who are objective that no person has done more to preserve General Lee's memory and his place in history than Hoover Adams.

Hoover has dozens of stories about General Lee. My favorite is an experience the General had in World War I. He was leading his company in a particularly fierce battle when a barrage of enemy artillery hit all around him. The fighting was extreme, and it came unexpectedly. Lee called out for his men to find a trench and stay in it. He saw a deep crater, started running for it, and fell right on top of a black soldier. They began to talk and his fellow soldier told him he was from Dunn. Lieutenant Lee was so overcome that he immediately threw his arms around him and vowed that when he returned home, he was going to find this fellow soldier. Once back, he tried, but no one had ever heard of a black American from Dunn who had been fighting close to where Lee had been in the war. General Lee joked through the years that he had been saved by an angel in that episode and the angel had been from Dunn.

In the beginning, doing this project seemed like a good retirement transition, but its daunting nature quickly became evident. It could not have been accomplished without the help of General Lee's nephew, Harry Driver. Harry has been enormously generous with his time and in being involved in our research efforts. He meticulously preserved all of General and Mrs. Lee's personal memorabilia over the years. We would never have been able to relive General Lee's life had not Harry saved it exactly as he did. Harry's adoration for his Uncle Bill is much in evidence, even going back to when he was a youngster. One story I happened upon illustrates their mutual admiration. Harry was heading to work at his after school job at the A & P food store when he saw General Lee round the corner in his staff car. The General stopped, got out of his car, hugged Harry, and asked where he was going. Then he took off his hat—with those two gigantic stars pinned to it—put the hat on Harry's head, saluted, got back in the big Army car, and drove off. From the very moment I wrote Harry almost a year ago, he pledged his cooperation—even in the midst of an incredibly busy schedule. Special thanks also to his faithful secretary, Pat, who has gone out of her way to assist.

Thanks, too, to all those who have talked to Kathryn, my able research assistant. To say that I could never have done this without her would have to be the understatement of all time. Of course, she is my niece, but I really didn't know her before this project began. Now, after thousands of e-mails, faxes, mailings, and phone calls, we have a rapport that is not often experienced. She is terrific; a friend asks when I mention her, "How is your alter-ego?"

In the beginning, there was so much material that it was dismaying. The General and Mrs. Lee had a wonderful hobby of preserving their memories by pasting their pictures in scrapbooks throughout their lives. In one of his last letters to Mrs. Lee from overseas, General Lee mentioned putting that letter in their scrapbook. In order to understand their lives by looking at the pictures, we had to look at everything. I did not have a clue as how to even begin. Kath began making photocopies in chronological order and sending them to me. The quantity of material was inundating, and sometimes I said there was no way we could get at it all. But Kath persevered and it began to become clearer. Putting the book together is a story in itself. Kathryn's constant encouragement—"Uncle Jerry, we can do it!"— has brought us to where we are today.

My thanks to James Blue. James has been a mentor to me in the project. Before I made a final decision on proceeding, I called and talked to James and then he sent me a wonderful packet of material that inspired me to push on. Later on, I made a trip to Dunn and we spent a day together going to some of the historical sites and visiting the 82nd Airborne Division. I listened to him; it was like living history. I asked James how he decided to become a paratrooper. He said it was while watching one of the airborne demonstrations arranged by General Lee. James was standing on the side of the field and suddenly the planes came into view. He said, "The lump in my throat was as big as an apple and my heart was racing. Billowing from the side door of the huge transport were bodies filling the sky—they looked like balloons. Suddenly, I knew in my heart my destiny was to be a paratrooper. As those four huge planes emptied their cargo, I knew that General Lee was one of them. Growing up, I had heard stories of him. He was Dunn's most famous soldier. He had been in World War I and everybody said he was humble, fearless, and independent. I had no idea that he would forever be known as the Father of the Airborne. Little did I realize that General Lee's destiny would in its own way prove to be the catalyst for events that I would experience first hand over the next several months." In my way of thinking, First Sergeant James Blue is a national treasure. He has lived what we talk about and being in the presence of my fellow paratrooper makes me very grateful.

Thanks to Ms. Pearsall, my third grade teacher, for her generosity in time and for her thoughts about her Aunt Dava. I remember in particular what a wonderfully kind teacher she was. She beams when she talks about her Uncle Bill and Aunt Dava. "After I got out of school, Aunt Dava asked me to come live with them. I wanted to get a job teaching, and she said they were looking for teachers in Dunn and that I should put in my application. Eventually I did get a job and stayed briefly with them while I was looking for my own place. We had many wonderful days. Uncle Bill was a wonderful chess player and we had a great time. One day Aunt Dava told me that Uncle Bill was worried that young men wouldn't be coming to see me because he was sick. This was so typical of him, always concerned about everyone else but himself."

General Lee was a spectacular writer. Constantly, I have been struck by his own good education at Dunn High, and it reinforces pride in my own. When I talked to my friend Iris Knell, of George Mason University, who helped me with some editing, I said: "Please don't let me have punctuation and grammatical mistakes. The thought that my teachers—Ms. Dixon, Mrs. Pridgen, Mrs. Grantham, Mrs. Wilson, Mr. Denny, and scores of others—would be displeased would be too much for me to bear."

Thanks to all my readers, those wonderful friends that I ask to read material in the beginning to see if I was heading in the right direction: June Hawes from Willcox, Arizona; my good Army buddies, Jane Livingston and Colleen Haselbusch from Sierra Vista, Arizona; and Colonel Linda Carter, who has already suggested who should play General Lee in the movie; and, of course, Meg and Rachael Autry, two very voracious readers ready at a moment's notice to tell their Dad what they think. And, to Gavin Jacobson, M.D., who constantly asked, "How is that book coming?"

Thanks to my wonderful wife, who has persevered and encouraged me to continue at the most difficult of times. She has been like a cheerleader. From the very beginning, when I was trying to decide whether to attempt the project or not, she would say, "Why not? You love Dunn, you love the Airborne, this is a perfect marriage." And, of course, all who know her will understand that it has taken an unusual patience for Ms. Neatnik to tolerate my messes.

Thanks to Sue Knopf for the cover and book design. She has not only been the epitome of a professional, but has become a friend and mentor and my Macintosh guru.

Thanks to Horace and Becky Pope, my good friends from Dunn who have encouraged me in the project and have been my companions at the celebration over the years.

Thanks to my stupendous brothers for their constant sense of goodwill.

Thanks to Pat Pope of the Lee Commission who has been so helpful in his advice. Pat told me this great story about Mrs. Lee: "For many years after General Lee died, all of my experiences were extremely good with her although I didn't know her very well. She would get after the neighborhood kids sometimes for running through her flower beds and the normal things that kids do. I figured that she missed the General a great deal and in many ways was still in the grieving process. Then my family bought the house behind her, the old Tilghman place. We had one of the heinz variety dogs but we really loved the dog and he seemed to take a shine to Mrs. Lee. One day he was missing and we looked for him everywhere; and, finally, as I was coming home, Mrs. Lee came out to ask had we lost anything. I told her it was old Buck. She motioned for me to come over and we went into the back of her house; and, there he was, on her sofa with his paws sticking straight up into the air."

General Lee loved North Carolina State University. The only person I know who loves the Wolfpack as much is my nephew, Delone Autry. He has been invaluable in giving feedback as to our progress.

And, certainly thanks to all the members of the Lee Commission for their foresight in preserving General Lee's memory: Hoover Adams, Jesse Alphin, Tim Brown, Walter Dafford, Eugene Driver, Harry Driver, Tim Driver, Keith Finch, Oscar Harris, Pat Pope, Ray Whitaker, and Tammy Williams.

Thanks to the University of North Carolina Archives, North Carolina State University, with special thanks to Maurice Toler, Archivist; Ms. Brookie Stewart of Erwin; Mrs. Iva and Mr. Talmage V. Capps and Mr. Graham Henry of Dunn; Mrs. Tula Satterfield of New Bern; and Mr. Ambrose Lee of Benson.

Preface

As a youngster heading to Dunn High, I can remember seeing, morning after morning, the historical marker on West Broad commemorating something significant. I didn't pay much attention at the time, but somehow that marker burned itself into my memory. In fact, memory must have played a part when the First Sergeant of the 118th Airborne Military Police Company at Fort Bragg said to me in my first assignment : "Chaplain, there are three reasons you have to go airborne. Number one is that you will best be able to serve my soldiers. I'm not having a 'leg' as my chaplain. Secondly, if you are going to hang around Fort Bragg and put up with all this hassle, you might as well make a little extra money. And, most importantly," he went on, "the man who started it all is from your hometown."

Years later, when I was in the 1/501st Airborne Infantry Battalion of the 101st Airborne Division in Vietnam, I would brag about the fact that it all began with a country boy from Dunn, North Carolina. The 501st was the original parachute battalion of the Army, and that significance was not lost on me. My sojourn as a member of the famed 501st was during the last year it would be airborne. (The next year, it became an air assault division. Later on, another Dunnite, Clarence Corbett, whose dad had been our family doctor, followed me in the same unit.)

Originally, I had planned to write a biography of General Lee, or at least something close, but early in my research, I came to realize that I couldn't possibly capture his life's story in a few months—too much to read, too many interviews to do. As I was investigating, trying to make the decision whether to attempt it or not, I traveled to the 82nd Airborne Division Memorial Museum to see their collection of books. And then, Harry Driver was so kind as to take me to his home and show me the pictures of his Uncle Bill. On my trip back to California, the thoughts began to germinate and the idea of a "coffee table book" was born. In my mind's eye, I could see every family in my hometown having one on their coffee table—-a picture book about General Lee next to the wedding album.

It was not possible to merely go through pictures, rather, through albums, as General and Mrs. Lee from their earliest days had kept picture albums and scrapbooks as the record of their lives. It seemed only appropriate that this theme be maintained for the reader. The "coffee table" book is an interim attempt to do something special for the tenth anniversary of the General William C. Lee Airborne Museum and commemorate what would have been his one hundredth birthday. The biography is still to come. Stay tuned.

Contents

INTRODUCTION

The thoughts of writing about General Lee started in March 1994 as I wandered through the General Lee Museum. The museum is his old homeplace and exemplifies not only the esteem of an entire community but the amazing foresight of the General Lee Commission in establishing such a wonderful tribute. Alone, I was simply overwhelmed with the idea that there is so much about this uncommon man that should be told. As I read his famous Rendezvous With Destiny speech, I immediately thought, "This great use of words was fostered right at Dunn High School by some wonderful predecessor to Ms. Irene Dixon." Seeing in picture form the events of the Airborne, it became apparent that here was a story just waiting to be told. Because of my knowledge of the military, I knew that this tale was not a simple matter of one man who was the project officer for a new military war strategy.

Great accomplishments in life are usually centered in someone who can look into the future. Bill Lee certainly didn't invent the Airborne, but he provided the drive, the impetus, the insight, and the vision. Most things noteworthy in the early airborne days began and were moved along by Bill Lee. He worked himself to death—long days and nights without rest and sleep, not eating properly. And, let's don't leave out Dava Johnson Lee. She played a gigantic part in the drama, and therein lies much of the story—who does a husband talk to when there are problems, when he doesn't want to share his fears, suspicions, and innermost doubts? His wife.

Affectionate Anonymity

During my twenty-nine years in the Army, I said to people dozens of times: "The Father of the Airborne is from my hometown." More likely than not, the listener gave me the "Nobody's at home" look. After pouring over tons of paperwork, reviewing countless documents among General Lee's private papers—the Army Department of History archives, interviews, all the literature (or all I could find), I have a story to reveal.

General William Carey Lee has been the object of what might well be called "affectionate anonymity." Every history of the military acknowledges him as the "Father of the Airborne." But, more likely than not, the various accounts end there. I want to set the record straight in telling the story of this unusual man. There are many reasons for the historical vagueness. One is that on the eve of the decisive turning point of World War II, Bill Lee's overworked and overburdened heart gave out; and, in war, more than at any other time, we are a people who relish the finished job. Consequently, the historical crown of notoriety and fame is reserved for the combatant. Since Bill Lee stopped just short of the completed task, he never received his just due.

There's no doubt about it: much of the success achieved on D-Day by airborne troops was the direct result of the work of this distinguished warrior. Bill Lee's story is not a revisionist history. It is important that he take his rightful place as one of the military giants of his time, right up there with Ike, Bradley, Ridgway, and Taylor, at the very least. He deserves it. In his writings, I have been overwhelmed with his graciousness even to those who would disregard his rightful place or attempt to outmaneuver him for their personal aggrandizement. Who they were is irrelevant because General Lee never attached importance to petty issues that often seemed to engulf others.

Early in my research, I discovered a simple fact: Bill Lee's place in history is somewhat ambiguous because of Bill Lee himself. He was unpretentious and modest to a fault. Making over him and telling of his greatness embarrassed him no end. Only after death did many deserved honors come to him. Had he been alive, he would never have accepted them. When his hometown had a victory celebration in June of 1942, he commented in a letter to the mayor, "I feel very humble for your plans to include me in the program for your four day victory celebration. I do not consider myself in any way entitled to the honor which you propose for me and if I had my way about it, I would suggest that the General Lee part of the program be eliminated. I think that my home folks have exaggerated my rank, my job, and my importance, out of all proportion to what it should be."

The General's love for his hometown is an inspiration that none of us who share that affection can ever take lightly and it's reason enough to honor him in the way we do. He deserves it mightily. In the same letter he went on to say, "On the other hand, in view of the fact that it is your opinion that my presence might add in some way to the success of your celebration, I cannot bring myself to refuse to accept this great honor. If the celebration were to be held at any place other than in my hometown and by my own folks, I would not think of accepting it." Like Washington and Jefferson before him, he always wanted to come back home; and, when he was finally laid to rest, it was among those he loved the most.

The shared experiences of the Airborne and our mutual love and appreciation for our wonderful little town had some influence on my wanting to tell General Lee's story. Interestingly, in my research, I've found some evidence that we are distant cousins—my mom was a Lee; her father Jason was a Freewill Baptist preacher.

Different Perspectives

In pouring over thousands of pages of notes and background history and learning an enormous amount about the Airborne (one of the great loves of my life), I've discovered something that must be mentioned and reinforced: even men of great integrity see things from individual perspectives. As someone has said, "A person's perception is his reality." In other words, once the facts are in, they may be changed by the perception of the one who is telling the story—the same story, the same tale, the same experience, the same historical event differs in each person's perspective.

Chronology of Events

General Lee's story is a novel—a country boy from North Carolina who entered the military to go to World War I. Like the rest of the country, young Bill Lee was somewhat ambivalent about what was going on in that far-off land. Having gone to college, at both Wake Forest and North Carolina State and taken a bride, he went off to war. Serving in the trenches and facing death as a common way of life, he not only performed admirably, but was so cool under fire that after the war he remained in Germany in an official capacity as the de facto mayor of a small town.

Returning to the States and to his young bride, he wrestled with where to cast his lot—to choose the military as a career or pursue his love of the land. His love of country, wanderlust and a sense of his "place to stand" won out. He went on to a stint at North Carolina State teaching, then to Panama, where he discovered he was good at the profession of arms. A succession of assignments and schools followed. He came home at every opportunity. He went to France. Bill saw with his own eyes the failure of the Treaty of Versailles and the aggressive military bearing of the Germans. Their parachute training captured his imagination. Bill Lee was ever the tactician; the infantryman. Bill and Dava took advantage of their circumstances to travel. Returning to the States, Bill attempted to convince others of the new concept of the airborne and air infantry. At heart, Bill Lee was now the consummate professional—loving soldiers, understanding the need for training, while desperately wanting to contribute to a prepared military. The Lees moved to Washington, DC, for his last assignment before returning home.

Major Lee could have been content to accept the lack of interest in his ideas, but this was not his way, and he tried to convince the military decision makers about the great possibilities of airborne, vertical envelopment, and moving infantry by air. No one would listen. Undaunted, Bill Lee, crusader, charged ahead and talked to anyone who would pause. In a prophetic quirk of events, President Franklin Delano Roosevelt, while watching one of the old newsreels at his home at Hyde Park, New York, saw the Germans performing airborne operations. He was intrigued and wanted to know more: specifically, whether our own military had airborne capability. As the military leadership scrambled to respond to the President, Bill Lee became their answer.

Major Bill Lee was given the airborne project. Pursuing it with dogged determination, he employed his characteristic charm to move it along. The British were to later tag him with the description, "the Yank with the courtly manners." He pioneered a test platoon of soldiers, established the first battalion, and wrestled often with the disappointment of decisions made.

Bill, like the rest of the country, was swept up in wartime events. He worked around the clock to develop and steer the training of the airborne units in the direction of preparing for war. He fought against overwhelming odds for the divisional concept of airborne, enlisting the British in his ideas and possibilities. He converted others with his enthusiasm, mentored them, and for many became a father figure.

The Citizen Soldier

Bill Lee was an outsider in the system—a citizen soldier; not one of the elite. A letter from Bill's former boss, chief of infantry General George Lynch, on August 27, 1942, is very telling:

I was deeply moved by your generous letter Aug. 19. I rate my own part in the airborne project at a much lower value than you have accorded me. For I know of no project in expansion of the army where success depended as completely on the officer in charge as the paratroop airborne development. You know how constantly the threat hung over our heads of having the project removed from our jurisdiction. A threat which would have been realized except for the efficiency of which it was handled. It must be a source of extraordinary satisfaction to you to have brought about a development which had so many obstacles thrown in its path. It so often happens that the process of things to come is a transformation of war with only the satisfaction of saying, 'I told you so.' A very poor satisfaction indeed, after the event has demonstrated the disastrous results of neglect in keeping abreast of the times.

Your career has been of unusual interest to me. Only last January the War Department seemed uncertain as to whether they should promote you to a colonel and seven months later finds you a major general. I know of no promotion which has been so richly deserved and for which the country stands to reap a greater profit. I can see it will not be long now before you are moved to a theater of operations since the air divisions will necessarily be in the vanguard of any offensive. God be with you.

Constantly facing formidable opposition, Bill never lost sight of his objective. Championed by sources outside himself for promotion, he moved into command and struggled regularly with shortages of supplies, equipment, and men during the fledgling development of the Airborne. The entire paratrooper movement might have been shot down in bureaucratic flames had not it been for this trench fighter.

Now a general, Bill Lee was constantly on the road between Georgia, Washington, and England, with an occasional respite to his hometown. Despite all his painstakingly nurturing hard work, the first airborne division command appeared to go to someone else. Gracious beyond imagination, never stopping to lament or acknowledge the slights, the determined general used the forces of events to leverage his positions, projecting the airborne along. Almost by default, he got his division, the command prize of the infantryman, when the designated division was formed into two separate divisions.

Fighting the battles of bureaucratic stupidity or intentional disregard, he experienced disappointment in not being the first airborne division deployed to Europe. Instead of languishing in this shameful oversight, he applied his favorite Abraham Lincoln principle, "I will prepare myself and when the time is right, I will be ready." Turning the lemon experience into lemonade, he used the time to train the 101st Airborne Division to be the very best in the world. Analyzing early airborne operations and learning from them, he trained recruits, dealt with the growing pains of his division, and its deployment, all the while planning for combat. Finally, he traveled to England with his "Screaming Eagles" and personally wrote the airborne invasion doctrine for D-Day.

General William C. Lee suffered a heart attack on February 5, 1944, having worked himself almost literally to death. His rich legacy did not end with his heart attack. I, and literally thousands like me, both in war and peace, were and continue to be recipients of all he would accomplish.

A Final Note

I have tried desperately not to make General Lee a saint. It has been very hard. As I have studied his papers, the comments of his contemporaries about him, the interviews of those who knew the General and Dava and their family life, and especially his letters, I have occasionally felt intrusive. Consequently, as I have selected pictures and other material, I have been extremely careful not to violate this sacred privilege I've been given.

General Lee adds new meaning to letter writing. He wrote literally hundreds of letters to his friends, the famous, his compatriots, all ranks—I have been overwhelmed. An incredibly private man, almost painfully modest and refreshing in a world obsessed with media and celebrity, this historical figure is a penetrating star in the historical galaxy. To compare him to modern day generals and their million-dollar memoirs is to find a pride almost beyond description. I will forever be indebted for this opportunity to get to know him. This book is your conduit, I hope you'll get to know him as well as I have. When I started this project, I remember almost absent-mindedly saying one day, "Bill, I need your help." I think he gave it.

Paratroopers have an all-purpose affirmation for one another—a greeting, a farewell, an amen. When they say "Airborne!" they are declaring membership in an elite group meticulously trained to conquer danger. And in those two proud syllables is tribute to the man who made it all possible—General Bill Lee … Airborne!

Just Plain Bill

Eldredge and Emma Massengill Lee had six sons: Eugene, Marion, Robert, Henry, William and Edward (not pictured) and one daughter, Emma. One child, George Royster Lee, born September 12, 1902, died two days later.

1

Early Life

William C. Lee was born on March 12, 1895 to Emma Massengill Lee and Eldredge Lee. The Lees moved to Dunn soon after the town was started; and, through the years Eldredge served as town mayor, alderman, justice of the peace, assistant judge of the local recorder's court, U. S. Commissioner, and librarian in the North Carolina Senate. According to his obituary,

> Mr. Lee was one of the pioneer citizens of Dunn and had been closely allied with the religious, civil and educational life of the town. He took an active interest in his Church and Sunday school and in good government. He could always be found standing for and fighting for those things which tended for the best interest of the masses. He was public spirited and had no small part in the building of Dunn and was often called Squire by the locals.

It is likely that as a youngster Bill worked with his dad in the hardware store, as in those days, the hardware store was a provider of services, with tools and implements supplied by the store. He also worked in the tobacco and cotton fields; and, thus began his love of the land.

Bill's older brother Gene, while doing civil engineering field work in Mexico, was shot by a bandit and paralyzed for life, but returned to Dunn to become one of its most prominent citizens. Gene was particularly well liked, and a portion of a letter written to the *The Dunn Dispatch* eulogized him like this:

> ... it could be truly said that he was a man who lived by the side of the road and was a friend to man. He could have been rich in money had he worked as hard for Gene Lee as he did for his county and town. But he died much richer than any amount of money could have made him with a world of friends.

Bill seemed touched by this letter. He was very close to all his family but especially to Gene.

Willie Lee was a remarkably gifted athlete and excelled especially in baseball. He chose to attend Wake Forest College, probably influenced by his family's association with the First Baptist Church, and may have received a baseball and football scholarship. He found Wake Forest enjoyable, but decided to transfer to North Carolina State since Wake Forest did not have ROTC and Bill thought he might be interested in the military.

Since job opportunities were not plentiful in his hometown, Bill worked for a time as teacher and principal at Turlington School between Coats and Erwin, North Carolina.

Dava and Bill were high school sweethearts and were married on June 5, 1918 in Chattanooga, Tennessee. Why they chose Chattanooga for the ceremony is unknown, but they may have decided on a combination wedding and honeymoon there as Bill soon went off to war.

Childhood Schooling

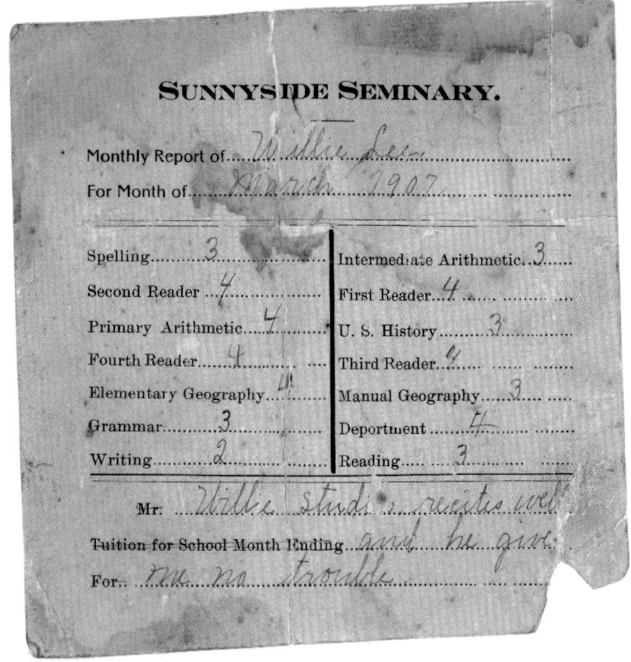

SUNNYSIDE SEMINARY.

Monthly Report of Willie Lee

For Month of March 1907

Spelling	3	Intermediate Arithmetic	3
Second Reader	4	First Reader	4
Primary Arithmetic	4	U. S. History	3
Fourth Reader	4	Third Reader	4
Elementary Geography	4	Manual Geography	3
Grammar	3	Deportment	4
Writing	2	Reading	3

Mr. Willie studies recites well

Tuition for School Month Ending and he gives

For me no trouble

ABOVE: Bill Lee attended Sunnyside Seminary before entering Dunn High School. He is in front on the left.

BELOW: 1911 Dunn High School baseball team. Bill is number 6—the shortstop.

Young Bill Saves the Game and Starts a Sports Story Spanning 15 Years

AUGUST 21, 1915
CHARLOTTE, N.C. NEWS

Special to the News

Red Springs, August 20—Did you hear about that game Wednesday. It was some game, Guess when you were a boy about 12 or 13 years old you used to steal out behind the barn and read a certain weekly publication called the Tip-Top Weekly, in which the leading character was that beloved hero, Dick Merriwell and wonder if ever you would see his likeness in the flesh. Well, reader, we have a Dick Merriwell in this town now. he made himself shown yesterday. Only got his chance when it as most needed in the game which was to cinch the championship in Eastern Carolina. He answers to the name of Bill Lee, is a native of Dunn, N.C., and is also a junior at Wake Forest. It was in the ninth with two down, Jim Fox on first, score 3 to 2 in favor of Red Springs, two strikes, three balls on strain, Whitey Glazner shot a fast one down the alley and "bimb" it looked good for the circuit, but our hero, turning at the crack of the bat and running at full speed toward the flying sphere stabs it in his bare hand, saving the game and cinching the championship for Red Springs in the Eastern Circuit.

The fans made a collection amounting to $10, not so bad for a town of only 1,500 people, and in the cotton belt, too. He not only saved the game but he batted an even 1000, and scored the first run himself, and his hit scored the next one. That boy will always have a home in this town.

If he keeps up the pace he is going now he will root some man out of a job in the big show when he gets some more experience, for he has all the natural requirements of a big leaguer. We hope to see him go up some day if he chooses baseball as his vocation in life.

AUGUST 20, 1930
GREENSBORO, N.C. DAILY NEWS

Breaks of the Game

(*From an article about Tom DeVane's search for information about old time North Carolina amateur baseball.*)

Well, Tom, thanks for the ancient history, thanks a great deal, but can you tell me when you old timers are going to get together and send me the name of the boy who made that catch under the edge of the school house at Red Springs one afternoon years ago. This corner hereby offers a reward for the name of that player. If you have it—don't write, telegraph, collect.

AUGUST 21, 1930
GREENSBORO, N.C. DAILY NEWS

Breaks of the Game

The lost has been found. Kill the spotted heifer calf, cull the pen for prime shoats, clean out the barbecue pit for fresh hickory coals are coming, tap the shelf for brandied peaches, fix me a lot of corn bread—one inch thick with golden crust patted on top by expert fingers—and get that coffee ready.

The following telegram (Western Union) explains all, tells all.

RED SPRINGS, AUG. 20, 1930
W.N. COX, SPORTS EDITOR
GREENSBORO DAILY NEWS.

THE CATCH SPOKEN OF IN YOUR COLUMN WAS MADE IN GAME BETWEEN LUMBERTON AND RED SPRINGS THAT CLINCHED EASTERN CAROLINA CHAMPIONSHIP - STOP - IT WAS THE THIRD OUT IN THE NINTH INNING TWO MEN ON BASE - STOP - WAS MADE BARE HANDED BY BOB LEE OF DUNN, N.C., WHO LATER WENT TO STATE COLLEGE AS INSTRUCTOR. SIGNED—J.A. LOVE JR.

AUGUST 22 1930
GREENSBORO, N.C. DAILY NEWS

Bill Lee Caught It

Messengers made a bee-line for the sports department of the Daily News yesterday morning bearing news that it was Bill Lee—not Bob—who made the catch in the game at Red Springs between that team and Lumberton for the Eastern Carolina title.

Tom DeVane, of Fayetteville, wrote in to say it was Bill and McDaniel Lewis, well known local sportsman, called to say it was Bill. Mr. Lewis, an old timer ball player in his own right, having put in three years at Carolina in 1912-14-15 and who later saw service in semi-pro ranks in this state and Florida, also says Bill Lee is now a Capt. in the Army and is stationed at Camp Meade, Md., where he has charge of a tank corps.

Sixteen year old memories are bound to slip. Bill Lee, formerly of Dunn, made the play. Everybody's happy now!

[*Note: After this article, Bill wrote in his album, "I wonder if I'll ever command a corps, 100,000 men or more!*]

SEPTEMBER 3 1930
GREENSBORO, N.C. DAILY NEWS

From Captain Bill Lee

Fort George G. Meade, Maryland

Sirs:

A couple of years ago while serving with my regiment in Panama, a friend of mine sent me a clipping … in which you had quite a bit to say about a ball game played in Red Springs, N.C., exactly 15 years ago this month. You particularly referred to a certain play made in that game, and you were eager for someone to recall the name of the player who made that play. As I am the man who made the catch your article brought back old memories and happy memories, but after a few days the incident was again forgotten.

But a few days ago when the same friend sent me a clipping from your column of August 20th in which you again requested some of the old timers to send you the name of the man who made the play, I decided to do my bit in getting ancient history straight.

I searched through an old, half-forgotten scrapbook that my sweetheart (who is now my wife) kept while I was a student at Wake Forest and N.C. State colleges, and I found an account of that play taken from the Charlotte News of August 20, 1915.

I am enclosing that clipping herewith. If it is of any interest or value to you, you are welcome to it.

Sincerely yours,
(Signed) WILLIAM (BILL) LEE
Capt., U.S. Army, First Tank Regiment

OPPOSITE LEFT: The championship Red Springs baseball tean for the East, 1915.

RIGHT: 15 years later, the story ended.

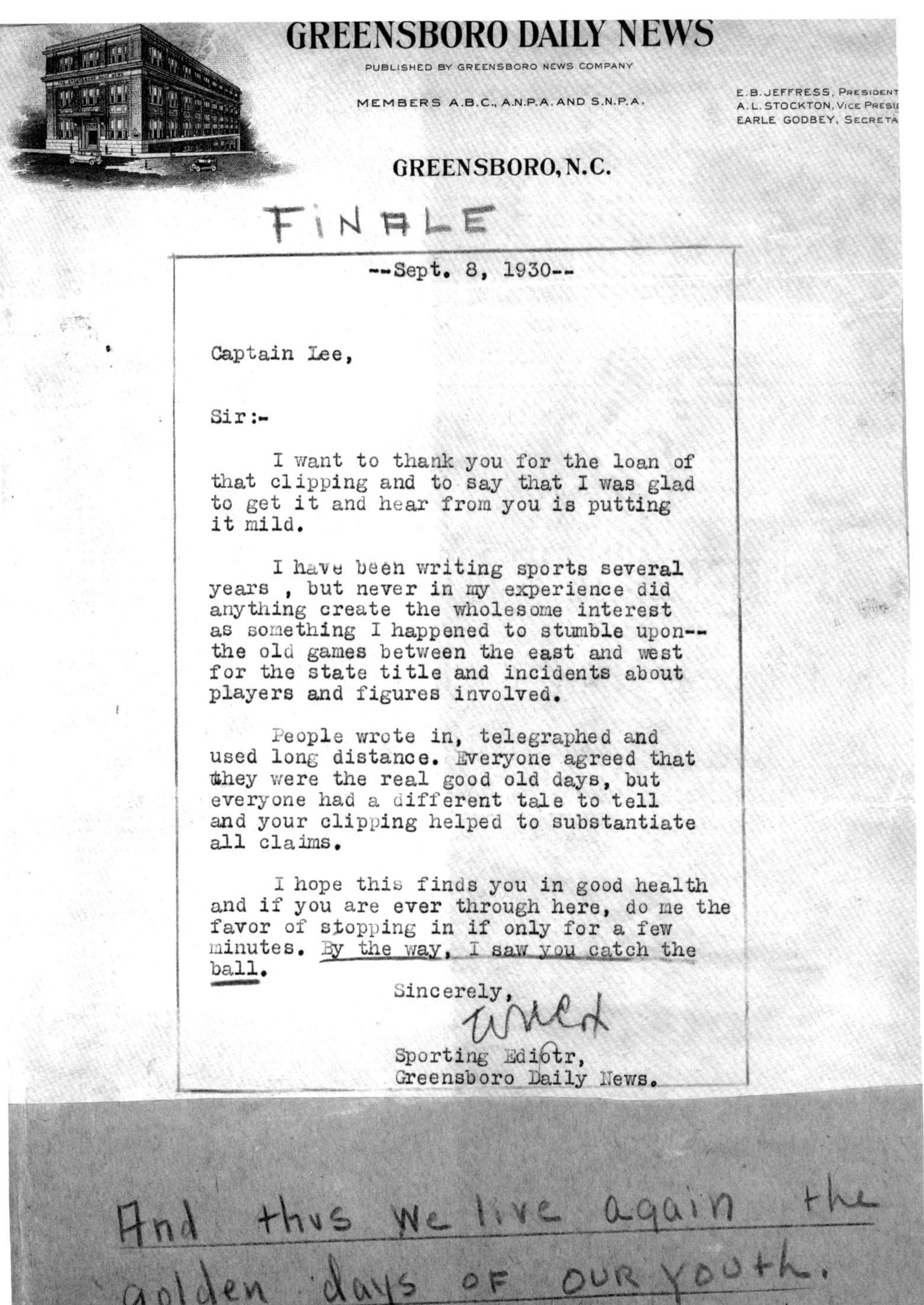

GREENSBORO DAILY NEWS
PUBLISHED BY GREENSBORO NEWS COMPANY
MEMBERS A.B.C., A.N.P.A. AND S.N.P.A.
E. B. JEFFRESS, PRESIDENT
A. L. STOCKTON, VICE PRESI[illegible]
EARLE GODBEY, SECRETA[illegible]
GREENSBORO, N.C.

FINALE

--Sept. 8, 1930--

Captain Lee,

Sir:-

I want to thank you for the loan of that clipping and to say that I was glad to get it and hear from you is putting it mild.

I have been writing sports several years , but never in my experience did anything create the wholesome interest as something I happened to stumble upon--the old games between the east and west for the state title and incidents about players and figures involved.

People wrote in, telegraphed and used long distance. Everyone agreed that they were the real good old days, but everyone had a different tale to tell and your clipping helped to substantiate all claims.

I hope this finds you in good health and if you are ever through here, do me the favor of stopping in if only for a few minutes. By the way, I saw you catch the ball.

Sincerely,
[signature]
Sporting Ediotr,
Greensboro Daily News.

And thus we live again the golden days of our youth.

Bill as a college sportsman

ABOVE:
Football at North Carolina State.

LEFT:
Baseball at Wake Forest.

Bill as a young man

ABOVE:
The college years at Wake Forest and N.C. State.

LEFT:
Bill in his United States Reserve uniform.

LOWER LEFT:
Dava, Bill's future wife.

Nov 9th 1918.

Actual order received while in front lines ~~North~~ East of Verdun just before the Armistice. W.E. Lee

Lt. Lee
G.C. #2.

Watch for troops coming from our left front. When these troops come in sight have all men leave trenches bringing their packs + squad rolls with them. Assembly at cross road where company split up the night we took the sector over.

Lt. Bolton

By runner
7 [illegible]

Notify G.C. #1 and G.C. #3 at once, also men in village of Chatillon.

Actual order received while in front lines east of Verdun just before the Armistice.

2
Lieutenant in World War I
1917-18

Bill Lee entered the military on August 15, 1917. He did initial training and traveled to France by way of a troop ship loaned to America by Great Britain.The conditions on the ship were ghastly. Many men suffered from dysentery and seasickness the entire way. Lieutenant Lee was immediately assigned to the 81st Infantry Division and was to see some of the most fierce fighting of the war in the battle of the Meuse-Argonne. The battle was part of a general engagement that pressed against the entire length of the German line from Verdun to the English Channel. About 1,200,000 Americans took part. When the drive ended, the war was over.

The cost of the American effort in World War I will never be entirely known. Americans killed in battle or dead of wounds numbered 53,407. Illness and other causes brought the total number of deaths to about 126,000. In several letters home, Lieutenant Lee described the war in rather graphic terms. He was proud of having served in the war, even while admitting doubts as to its lasting results.

Early Military Training

Lieutenant Lee actually began his training on June 2, 1917 at the Military Training Camp at Plattsburg, New York, studying infantry tactics. He received his Reserve Commission on August 15, 1917. He did additional training at Camp Jackson in South Carolina, at Fort Oglethorpe in Georgia, and in Chattanooga, Tennessee.

A letter from the trenches of World War I

LIEUTENANT LEE TELLS ABOUT WAR

In a Letter to His Father, Describes What a Modern Battle Really Is.

NOW IN GERMANY WITH ARMY OF OCCUPATION

Does Not Know When he Will Return to the States, But is Being Well Cared For.

A letter from Lieutenant William C. Lee, who is with the army of Occupation in Germany, to his father, Eldridge Lee, of Dunn:

American Army Occupation,
Mayen, Germany.
Dec. 29th, 1918.

I am hoping that your Christmas was a very happy one and that the New Year will bring with it all kinds of good things for you. I wish that I could have spent the holidays with the home people but that being impossible I made the best of it and after all had an excellent time.

You probably have learned from my recent letters to Gene and Mama concerning conditions here and of our daily life among the Germans. Sufficient to say that the German people treat us with the utmost courtesy and respect and I do not know of a single instance in which there has been friction between the Americans and civilians. The people of Lorraine and Luxemburg gave us a very enthusiastic reception when we marched through their countries but the Germans received us with doubt and suspicion. However they were not long realizing that we were not savages

I am hoping that your Christmas was a very happy one and that the New Year will bring with it all kinds of good things for you. I wish that I could have spent the holidays with the home people but that being impossible, I made the best of it and after all had an excellent time. …

Our regiment has been decorated by the French with the "Croix de Guerre" with palms, for gallantry in the battles of the Marne and the Argonne. This is the highest honor given by the French and we were one of the few American regiments to receive it. Quite an honor and I am proud to have belonged to such a regiment. …

The popular civilian conception of a battle is quite different from the real thing. The average civilian has an idea that a fight is a glorious charge, with colors flying, bands playing, horsemen madly dashing to and fro, handsome young officers leading their men to victory with flashing words, and a YMCA secretary waiting at the end with hot chocolate and cigarettes. It is all wrong; particularly, the part about the YMCA secretary.

What really happens is this: some dark rainy night (it's sure to be raining) your battalion is ordered to take over a certain sector of the front line. Then the battalion is hiked all night in the rain and sleeps in the woods until the next day. It rains all day and, of course, the rations fail to show up.…

The companies and platoons are separated and enter the long communicating trenches leading to the front lines....

Fritz immediately opens up with his artillery and begins shelling the communicating trenches and the roads in the rear. He sends a few gas shells along as a welcome and then on top of the mud, the rain, and darkness, you have to don that instrument of torture technically known as a box respirator or gas mask....

If you are lucky, you get two meals a day consisting of corned beef, hardtack, and coffee. If you have only ordinary luck you get one meal a day, menu same as before. If you are neither lucky nor unlucky you have to make out with a canteen of water, à la tranchée.

After several days of rain, the sun might come out for a while each day. During one of the short periods that the sun is shining, you will emerge from your hole and promenade down the trench to some nice warm corner to dry out and take a smoke. You make yourself as comfortable as possible, pull out your Bull Durham and say to yourself that it is not so bad after all. Then you discover that you have no papers and your matches are all wet. To crown your misfortunes, the warm sun has brought to life millions and millions of animals that suddenly begin to bite and crawl all over your body. You rise to your feet, scratch like the dickens and exclaim: "Hell! I've got the cooties." Oh how many times I have heard those fatal words.

It is characteristic of the American not to stay downhearted very long and under any circumstances so you console yourself with the thoughts that your relief is

due that night and you will go back for a nice long rest. But when night comes do you get a relief? I say not! Instead you get an order that your platoon will go over the top at five AM the next morning after sixty minutes of artillery preparation and take hill number so and so. What a great and glorious feeling. NOT! Your company commander pays you a visit and through him you learn that a big drive is to be launched next morning all along the line.

In the excitement of getting ready you forget about your half starved wet and cootie bitten body and manage to live ten years during one night. A heavy artillery preparation is something that can't be described. Neither can you describe your own sensations. But after many long minutes, the zero hour eventually arrives, the barrage lifts and over you go. It is daylight by this time. The men in small groups, single file, pass through the wire and you find yourself in no-man's land. The boche artillery opens up. They pour shells in on you in quantities, qualities and varieties that you never before knew existed.

Then instead of the highly colored romantic descriptions of a grand and glorious charge, you see men scurrying for shell holes and any other kind of holes that may be convenient. Maybe the shelling will ease up a bit before long and you start your men going forward again. This time you notice that you haven't got as many men as you had when you started. Gradually and cautiously you work your way forward occasionally pausing and hunting shelter when things get too hot. Pretty soon they open up on you with their machine guns and what a wicked sound those bullets have.

It is not long before you realize that you have got to put some of those guns out of action before you can advance. It may take all day to do and at night you are in no man's land. You decide to lay low all night holding on to what you've got and finish taking the hill next morning. You pick out a hole to try and rest but the high explosive shells keep coming. There is nothing that tears a man's nerves up like a long grilling night under shell-fire. You hear wounded men groan all night and a runner comes to you occasionally with the news that you have lost another sergeant. In one attack, I saw one shell kill fourteen men. It blew them to pieces.

Somehow you manage to survive the night and the next morning at daylight you move forward again. The Americans have a way of always "getting there." So you eventually capture the hill, send your prisoners back, and signal your aeroplanes the position of your front lines. You rally your men and find that more than half of them are missing. Majors and captains got killed as well as lieutenants and enlisted men and you might get word that you are not commanding your company or even your battalion. You try to eat but gas has made your throat so raw that you can't possibly swallow the captured German bread and jam, which is all you have. And it goes on like that . Your relief never comes. You are reinforced instead and ordered to continue the advance. Finally you are withdrawn, given a couple of days rest and sent to another sector where the dose is repeated.

This is what war is like today. But even at that, we took what came as a matter of course and expected nothing better. We knew what we were up against. We are not grumbling about the hardships we had to endure. It was worth it all to be able to say; "we helped lick the Huns." We are proud that we were in a fighting unit. We are glad that we came and we are going to be glad when we go back. Above all we are glad (emphatically so) that the war is over. It is true that we have our bright days and almost see the humorous side of things but the only man that enjoys it is behind the lines. If you ever hear a man say that he has been through a big fight and would like to go back again you can either put him down as a fool or a liar.

I hope the days of war have passed forever but if we should ever have another you will see America rise as one man, for our experiences over here have made us love and appreciate more than ever the greatest country that God ever blessed.

I didn't intend writing such a long letter and hope that it will not tire you. Write to me often. It has been almost three months since I have received mail but I keep writing and maybe eventually a letter from home will filter through. Love to the family.

Your son,

Willie

Co. C, 30th Infantry,

A.P.O. No. 791 American E. F.

That is what war is like today. But even at that we took what came as a matter of course and expected nothing better. We knew what we were up against. We are not grumbling about the hardships we had to endure. It was worth it all to be able to say; "We helped lick the Huns." We are proud that we were in a fighting unit. We are glad that we came and we are going to be glad when we go back. Above all we are glad (emphatically so) that the war is over. It is true that we have our bright days and almost see the humorous side of things but the only man that enjoys war is the man behind the lines. If you ever hear a man say that he has been through a big fight and would like to go back again you can either put him down for a fool or a liar.

I hope the days of war have passed forever but if we should ever have another you will see America rise as one man, for our experiences over here have made us love and appreciate more than ever the greatest country that God ever blessed.

Post World War I Mayen, Germany

3
Town Major, Mayen, Germany
1919

When the war ended, Germany, to abide by the treaty of Versailles, was governed in a transitional period by the Allies. The Americans established a system of zones in which each town had a Zone Major, much like a town mayor or administrator. Lieutenant Lee was selected to be the Major of the town of Mayen. Why he was chosen is somewhat of a mystery; we know he did not volunteer, as he was anxious to return home to his new bride and his family. The Lieutenant was young and apparently had shown an unusual flair for being patient, an ability to get along with people, and talent for leadership. However, there is a strong indication that selecting him was the attempt of someone at a higher level to convince him to remain in the military. America was about to disband its military and the assignment to Mayen would keep this capable Lieutenant enlisted.

It is obvious that many of the Germans in Mayen grew to appreciate Lieutenant Lee's efforts as Zone Major and that he was always fair. He seems to have had many advisors and was always one to listen to others' opinions. However, he was not above denying claims that he felt were unfair. His subtle humor can be noted in several of his opinions or judgments.

During his tenure as zone major in Mayen, Lieutenant Lee expected the time to pass quickly until Dava could join him, but with the ending of the occupation, this was not to be. In one brief moment, just before he learned that he would soon be released from this duty and be returning home, he wrote Dava and indicated that maybe the military was not the place for him. He was lonely for her and for his fellow townspeople.

In the time between leaving his post as town major and returning home, Bill visited much of Europe. In subsequent tours of duty, he and Dava would visit many of the same places, and he relished serving as her tour guide.

Mayen was a city of approximately 100,000 people when Lieutenant Lee became the Zone Major. Located on the edge of the Eifel Mountain region of Germany, it is well known in World War II history as the area where Hitler sent all of the older people. Yet because of their prowess in farming, they were feeding all of the German army by the end of the war. Mayen is approximately 20 miles from Trier, the oldest city in all of Europe; and, just a few hours north lie Paris, Belgium, and Luxemburg.

Mayen, Germany

ABOVE:
A large wall surrounds Mayen, and here Bill spent many hours looking over the city and writing letters to his family and Dava.

RIGHT:
Overlooking Mayen is a medieval castle, very much a part of the city. Bill took many pictures from the very top. Today, the castle holds a museum, but it contains no mention of this period in the history of the town.

BOTTOM:
The city of Mayen had a large, open square which was the center of activity for daily briefings for Lieutenant Lee's associates, including approximately a dozen Germans who assisted him in his duties. The square is still prominent today in the city of Mayen.

Mayen, Germany

LEFT:
Lieutenant Lee loved to take pictures. When he returned home, he and Dava would spend hours gluing and writing subjects and a brief history below the pictures. Dava kept scrapbooks of all their activities.

BELOW LEFT:
Surrounding Mayen are scores of vineyards. Here Bill stops to check out a barrel of wine.

BELOW RIGHT:
Bill strikes a pensive pose with his friend Pinkerton, a New Yorker. Bill jokingly said he hoped the folks from North Carolina did not find out he was palling around with a Yankee.

ABOVE LEFT:
WIth the Lieutenant is his best friend, Dr. Miller. Bill helped him a great deal, as the town depended upon the Americans for medical care for a time.

ABOVE RIGHT:
The Lieutenant experimented briefly with a mustache, it seems.

RIGHT:
Bill mentioned in a letter that their vehicles were the only ones in the 30th Infantry that ran all the time.

Zone Major of Mayen

As Zone Major, Lieutenant Lee settled claims made by the townspeople. This sampling of his decisions shows his fairness and sense of humor.

Office of Town Major, Mayen, Germany
Aug. 23rd, 1919
From: Town Major, Mayen, Germany.
To: The Burgemaster, Mayen, Germany
Subject: Publishing of notice in the local newspapers.

For the information of the citizens of Mayen in regard to billeting of troops, we are forwarding the following notice to you to have translated and published in the local newspapers.

It has been impossible to notify each householder of the number of officers and men that would be billeted with them. Each family is hereby notified that they can expect some soldiers, the number being based upon the number of people in the family, the number of rooms, and the number of beds. Upon presentation of a billeting order from the town Major the householder will immediately prepare places for the number of officers and men stated upon the billeting order. In case there are not enough beds to accommodate that number,places will immediately be prepared on the floors, in living rooms and parlors. In no case will soldiers be turned away when a billeting order is presented. In case of overcrowding, steps will immediately be taken by the Town Major to relieve such conditions and make it as comfortable for the householder as well as the soldiers.

William C. Lee, 1st Lieut., 30th Infantry.
Town Major, Mayen, Germany

Office of Town Major, Mayen, Germany
Aug. 23rd, 1919
From: Town Major, Mayen, Germany
Subject: Claim of Stadtgemeinde, Mayen, Germany

1. On the night of Dec. 31, 1918, soldiers celebrated the incoming of the new year by roping a statue of the Kaiser, tying the end of the rope to a truck and dragging it by the neck through the streets of Mayen, finally dumping it into the yard of a prominent citizen. It is common report among officers and men here that the deed was perpetrated by American soldiers. I believe that there is a possibility of this being true.

2. I have investigated the remains and find that his ears, nose, and moustache were knocked off. It was so broken and disfigured that the features are no longer recognizable. The bust was 1.55 meters high and weighed 2000 lbs. It was carved from stone and sat on a stone pedestal about two meters high.

3. The statue was presented to the city of Mayen in 1908 by the Mayen Stone Works. It was erected in the heart of the city for ornamental purposes. The city claims that this likeness of the Kaiser is no longer fit to occupy a pedestal. Whether or not this is due to the Kaiser's loss of prestige or the damage to his bust, I do not know. In either case the Americans are blamed as being the cause.

4. 3000 marks is claimed as the sum that it will take to replace the bust. Under the present conditions I do not recommend payment as I do not believe the Kaiser will ever regain enough prestige to set either himself or his statue on another pedestal.

5. Investigation failed to reveal the names or the organizations of the solders responsible. At that time there were over 30 organizations in Mayen and it was not practical to take the necessary steps to find the responsible ones.

William C. Lee, 1st Lieut., 30th Infantry.
Town Major, Mayen, Germany

Office of Town Major, Mayen, Germany
Aug. 23rd, 1919
From: Town Major, Mayen, Germany
To: Zone Major and R. R. and C, Officer, 3rd Div.
Subject: Claim of Peter Kreusch Sen.

1. After a careful investigation of the claim of Peter Kreusch Sen attached hereto, the following is submitted.

2. The statement of the claimant as to the cause of the damage is correct, in that he was struck by a motorcycle while trying to avoid a truck. It is not believed that the claimant was negligent, nor that the accident was the result of fault or negligence on the part of the driver of either the truck or the motorcycle, but rather that it was necessarily incident to military occupation. No evidence as to the identity of the individual or unit responsible can be found.

3. Doctor's bill and hospital bill are attached hereto. Also the statement of the doctor as to the injuries. From all evidence obtainable this is all the actual damage sustained by the claimant as he is no longer working and consequently did not lose any time on his work.

4. The claim of 50 marks for a tear in the trousers seems ridiculous and it is recommended not to consider allowance of any indemnity for this. There is no evidence available to show that he sustained the loss of the coat and contents at the hands of Americans as it is more likely that these were lost at the hospital, if at all.

5. It is recommended that claimant be paid 79 marks as indemnity for doctor's bill and hospital expenses and that the rest of his claim be disallowed.

William C. Lee,1st Lieut., 30th Infantry.
Town Major, Mayen, Germany

From: Office of Town Major, Mayen, Germany
Aug. 27, 1919
From: Town Major, Mayen, Germany
To: Zone Major 3rd Div., Andernach, Germany.
Subject: Claim of Widow Johann Boos.

1. Investigation shows that on the night of August 1st, 1919, the claimant was assaulted by two American soldiers. The evidence is fully covered by the attached statements of the claimant and witnesses. Claimant states that she reported same to M. P. Headquarters here but nothing was ever done about it.

2. I saw the woman myself a few days after the assault and she was badly beat up. I personally know that she was laid up nine days from the effects. She was given medical attention by the 30th Infantry infirmary.

3. The claim is for loss of wages for nine days. Seven marks per day is claimed. The woman is a widow and supports three children. She has no property and earns her daily bread by the sweat of her brow.

4. I do believe the damage to have been incidental to military occupation but as the guilty parties cannot be apprehended, I recommend payment of claim of 63 marks.

William C. Lee, 1st Lieut., 30th Infantry.
Town Major, Mayen, Germany

Lieutenant Lee Settles Claims

rom : Town Major, Mayen, Germany.

o : Zone Major, 3rd Div., Andernach, German

ubject : Claim of Stadtgemeinde, Mayen, Germany.

1. On the night of Dec. 31st. 1918.
elebrated the incoming of th
f the Kaiser, tieing the end
ing it by the neck through
umping it ito the yard of a
eport among officers and men
rated by American soldiers.
ility of this being true.

2. I have investigated t
ose and moustache were knock
igured that the features are
as 1.55 meters high and weig
stone and sat on a stone pede

3. The statue was presen

rom : William C. Lee, Town Major, Mayen, 1st Lieut. Inf.,

o : The Burgemaster, Mayen, Germany.

ubject : Publishing of notice in the local newspapers.

1. For the information of the citizens of Mayen in regard to
troops, we am forwarding the following notice to you to have t
published in the local newspapers.

"It has been impossible to notify each householder of the
officers and men that would be billeted with them. Ea
some soldiers, the
e family, the number of
of a billeting order i
ately prepare places fo
billeting order. In ca
ber, places will immedi
and parlors. In no ca
rder is presented. In e
taken by the Town Major

Office of Town Major
Mayen Germany
1 July 1919

60

From : Town Major, Mayen, Germany

To : Zone Major and R.R.and C.Officer 3rd Div.

Subject : Claim of Peter Kreusch Sen.

1. After a careful investigation of the claim of Peter
attached hereto, the following is submitted.

2. The statement of the claimant as to the cause of the
correct, in that he was struck by a morotcycle while trying t
a truck. It is not believed that the claimant was negligent,
the accident was the result of fault or negligence on the pa
driver of either the truck or the motorcycle, but rather tha
necessarily incident to military occupation. No evidence as
indentity of the individual or unit responsible can be found

3. Doctor's bill and hospital bill are attached hereto.
statement of the Doctor as to the injuries. From all eviden
this is all the actual damage sustained by the claimant as h
longer working and consequently did not lose any time on his

4. The claim of 50 marks for a tear in the trousers see
lous and it is recommended not to consider allowance of any
for this. There is no evidence available to show that he su
loss of the coat and contents at the hands of Americans as i
likely that these were lost at the hospital, if at all.

5. It is recommended that claimant be paid 79 marks as
for Doctor's bill and hospital expenses and that the rest of
be disallowed.

Town Major, Mayen, G

Zone Major, 3rd Div.

Claim of Widow Johan

Investigation show
laimant was assaulte
fully covered by th
d witnesses. Claima
eadquarters here but

I saw the woman my
badly beat up. I
s from the effects.
Infantry infirmary.

The claim is for
lay is claimed. The
ren. She has no pr
of her brow.

I do not believe
y occupation but as
I recommend payme

Mayen, Germany

LEFT:
Mayen's snowfall was measured in feet, not inches.

BELOW LEFT:
Statue of Kaiser Wilhelm I.

BELOW RIGHT:
Bill stands by the Mosel River. On the hills across the river are vineyards that fascinated Bill, a farmer at heart.

Denkmal
Kaiser Wilhelm I

ABOVE LEFT:
Lieutenant Lee lived with this family, the Spielbergers, while in Mayen. He commented that they treated him like a son.

ABOVE RIGHT and BELOW:
General "Black Jack" Pershing came to visit Lieutenant Lee on several occasions. His view that it was totally unacceptable to send untrained soldiers into battle had a profound effect upon Lieutenant Lee's entire military career.

Bill Travels

CLOCKWISE FROM ABOVE:
On the way to Berlin; at the Firth of Fourth; crossing the channel; Luxemburg.

Going Home

ABOVE:
Bill's last look at France.

BELOW:
Going home aboard the *Amerika*.

On board the "Amerika
en route home-
"Convalescing"

4
Early Stateside Military Life

1920-21

Lieutenant Bill Lee's return to the U. S. was a momentous occasion. Waiting for him was the love of his life, Dava. She met him in New York and they had a second honeymoon, and then spent several weeks in their hometown visiting family and friends.

There seems to be some evidence that Bill was seriously considering leaving the military. During this re-entry period, Bill's love of the land and his hometown was rekindled, and this coupled with his horrendous experiences in the war affected him enormously. Also, he could not easily forget how lonely he had been for Dava. However, Dava seems to have encouraged him to remain in the military, at least for a while, as she like the idea of traveling and had missed the opportunity to join him in Germany during the occupation.

Bill was assigned to Camp Jackson for a time and then seems to have gone on extensive maneuvers. During this time, Dava visited and they traveled. They had military quarters on post at Camp Jackson and seemed to have relished getting to know Columbia, South Carolina and the surrounding areas, making many friends.

San Antonio was a favorite site, and on one of their many adventures, they made a trip into Mexico. They also went as far as New Orleans and Colorado.

Dava's natural friendliness complemented Bill's boyish charm and this combination made them extremely popular. Their picture albums are filled with places they went and people they met.

As a follow-up to this assignment, Bill attended the officer's infantry basic course. This had to be an interesting period for Lieutenant Lee. He had been to war, had experiences that most of his classmates only talked about; and yet, as a seasoned warrior, he was being taught basic infantry tactics. But, true to form, all indications show that he contributed to the course in an exceptional manner in terms of his experience and positive attitude.

Camp Jackson

Camp Jackson

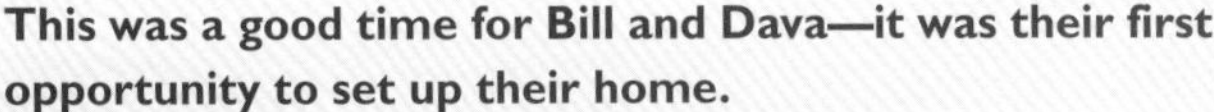

This was a good time for Bill and Dava—it was their first opportunity to set up their home.

LEFT and BELOW TOP and MIDDLE:
Dava and the Lees' post home.

BELOW BOTTOM:
Bill loved his dogs. This one, possibly named after a friend, was called Bob.

Camp Jackson

TOP LEFT:
On the polo field.

TOP RIGHT:
American Legion Parade; Camp Jackson band.

MIDDLE and BOTTOM RIGHT:
Bill gave this big artillery piece the affectionate name "Dixie." The "Dixie Girl" was in action for 90 consecutive days. In the bottom picture, Dava and a friend sit on "Dixie."

TOP LEFT:
Officers of the 46th Infantry at Camp Jackson, May 1920.

TOP RIGHT, MIDDLE:
Dava enjoyed herself immensely.

BOTTOM LEFT:
Several friends from Dunn visited and they often stayed in this cottage close to the river.

BOTTOM RIGHT:
While attending the Officer's Course at Fort Benning, the Lees lived in a little apartment in Columbus, Georgia.

Fort Benning

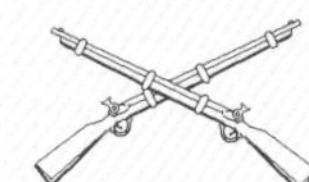

TOP LEFT: The Lieutenant had just bought his first set of "whites" and was showing them off.

TOP RIGHT, BOTTOM LEFT and RIGHT: A little time out for fishing.

TOP:
The proud possessor of a flivver.

BOTTOM:
Traveling from Eagle Pass to San Antonio, Texas in 1920.

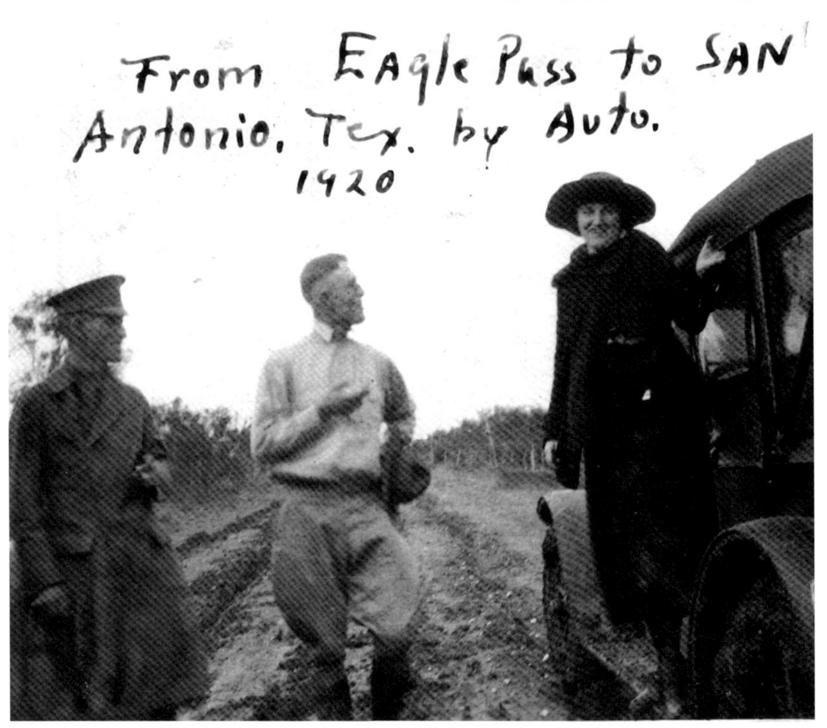

Camp Bullis, Texas

Tents at Camp Bullis.

Bill and Dava's camp on the Colorado, 1921.

More Travels

In their travels, the Lees visited New Orleans and Texas, including the Alamo, where they were very much impressed with the exploits of a fellow North Carolinian, Macajah Autry. Below, a favorite guesthouse called the Hacienda.

ABOVE:
Near Mexico City in 1921.

BELOW:
Down beneath the sheltering palms.

RIGHT:
In August 1921, Bill puts on "cits" (civilian clothes) for the first time since May of 1917. He was not permitted to enter Mexico in uniform.

A Visit to Mexico

Dava and Bill pose on the balcony of their Mexico City hotel and then show the view over the house tops.

Raleigh and North Carolina State College in those days were intertwined. Bill and Dava first had an apartment just off campus and then, for a while, just off Fayetteville Street.

5

Assistant Professor, Military Science & Tactics

N.C. State, 1922-26

The Lees' assignment to Reserve Officers Training Corps duty at North Carolina State was a dream come true. First of all, it enabled them to be close to their hometown. Not only could they visit, but Bill would have ample time to hunt and fish with his friends. Professionally, it also provided Bill an opportunity to teach many of the things he had learned at war.

Lieutenant Lee had been powerfully influenced by the philosophy of General Black Jack Pershing, who had made training of the American soldier in World War I a cornerstone of his policy. However, due to the rapidly collapsing allied forces, America was prematurely thrust into the war and General Pershing was never able to infuse training on a wholesale scale. Lieutenant Lee understood the ramifications of this failure, as he had seen first hand the loss of many of his fellow soldiers through their lack of basic knowledge. Many did not even know how to load their weapons. His assignment at State enabled him to make his small contribution to individual training.

These were unusual times for the military. The armed forces had dwindled to almost nothing and there was no real incentive for anyone to be in the service. The country was in an isolationist mood, making a military career almost an impossibility. Still, there were many North Carolina youngsters who had a natural patriotism and were motivated to try their hand at ROTC. And, of course, Lieutenant Lee had a special interest in the ROTC program because it had given him his start. He had a strong feeling that the country should be militarily prepared for any eventuality, which he instinctively knew would come in the future.

12 STATE COLLEGE CATALOG

DEPARTMENT OF MILITARY SCIENCE AND TACTICS

RESERVE OFFICERS TRAINING CORPS

Daniel Dixon Gregory, Lieutenant-Colonel, U. S. A., Retired, Head of the Department.

Nathaniel Lewis Simmonds, Captain Infantry, U. S. A., D. O. L., Assistant Professor of Military Science and Tactics.

John Henry Gibson, Captain Infantry, U. S. A., D. O. L., Assistant Professor of Military Science and Tactics.

Robert Edward Wysor, Jr., Captain Infantry, U. S. A., D. O. L., Assistant Professor of Military Science and Tactics.

William Carey Lee, First Lieutenant Infantry, U. S. A., D. O. L., Assistant Professor of Military Science and Tactics.

Lester Austin Webb, First Lieutenant Infantry, U. S. A., D. O. L., Assistant Professor of Military Science and Tactics.

Horace Carter Thomas, Staff Sergeant, U. S. A., Instructor.

It would have been easy to simply enjoy himself while at State, but Lieutenant Lee was sincerely interested in teaching his young charges, of which there were approximately seventy five. He served as the weapons officer. The ROTC Department didn't have any real military equipment, but Bill instituted a plan for caring for what few weapons they did have. They had a single tank—a display model that had been allowed to rust. Bill and his young ROTC cadets scrubbed and cleaned it until it shined like a beacon on the campus. Also, through Lieutenant Lee's initiative, a strict regimen of drill and ceremony was instituted.

Toward the end of his tenure at State, Bill was promoted to Captain, and upon his departure, Bill Lee was officially acknowledged as the most popular instructor in the Department of Military Science and Tactics.

In the approximately four years Bill and Dava were at State, they became involved in the Raleigh community and regularly attended Pullen Baptist Church. Bill was a substitute Sunday School teacher when he was in town, and he and the pastor developed a strong friendship that continued even after the Lees left Raleigh.

Bill and fellow instructors. Bill is now a regular army officer.

ROTC Summer Camp

A major part of ROTC training was the summer camp cycle. The camp was held at Camp McClellan in Alabama and Bill loved the training part of each summer. The camp cadre trained ROTC cadets from throughout the country. Bill and Dava became close friends with the Camp Chaplain, a Captain McNally, and Dava often stayed with Ms. McNally on her visits to see Bill. When he was building the Airborne, many of his former ROTC cadets served with him.

BELOW:
Camp Headquarters Staff at Camp McClellan.

General Pershing Visits Camp McClellan

General Pershing visits Lieutenant Lee's ROTC camp.

Enjoying Life in Raleigh

TOP LEFT:
Dava thrived at State and entered into the life with great vigor. Her best friend was the wife of a fellow ROTC instructor.

TOP RIGHT:
We were brave souls, Dava wrote, heading to Alabama to visit.

BOTTOM LEFT:
Dava loved to babysit for her friend. The child's name is Melanie.

BOTTOM RIGHT:
For a time, Bill and Dava shared a large house with another couple.

TOP LEFT:
Bill's all-time favorite outing: the North Carolina State Fair.

TOP RIGHT, MIDDLE, and BOTTOM LEFT:
The Lieutenant still found time for training his dogs and said that his friend Tom (TOP) was the best with dogs he had ever seen.

Bill Lee Is Promoted to Captain

PULLEN MEMORIAL BAPTIST CHURCH
HILLSBORO STREET AND COX AVENUE
RALEIGH, N. C.

JOHN A. ELLIS
PASTOR
RESIDENCE: 1808 PARK DRIVE
PHONES: RES. 1072-Y
STUDY 2896

R. M. WARREN
DIRECTOR OF STUDENT ACTIVITIES
OFFICE IN CHURCH BUILDING
PHONE: 2896

November 10th,1925.

Capt.W.C.Lee,
State College Station,
Raleigh, N.C.

Dear Will:

I congratulate you most heartily upon the honor that has come to you through your promotion to a captaincy. Of course I feel like congratulating the President also in this evidence of good taste and in his ability to recognize a solider when he sees one and his willingness to give honor where honor is due.

The news that you will be transferred from Raleigh is not at all welcome to your friends,but they will all rejoice at the larger field of service that will come to you through this honor.

With kindest regards to you and Mrs.Lee, I am,

Cordially yours,

J. A. Ellis

Bill was highly thought of by Pastor Ellis of the Pullen Memorial Baptist Church.

POPULAR R. O. T. C. OFFICER PROMOTED AND TRANSFERRED

Has Been Prominent in Campus Activities Since His Student Days

Lieutenant W. C. Lee, U. S. A., who for the past three years has been stationed at State College, has received notice from the War Department of his promotion by President Coolidge to the rank of Captain, the commission to date from October 27. Captain Lee, it is understood, will finish the school year at State College, after which he will be ordered to duty with the Tank Corps, with headquarters at Fort Meade, Maryland...

Captain Lee was assigned to duty at State College in 1922, coming to the college after graduation from the Infantry School at Fort Benning, GA.

Following the reduction of the military forces after the war, which necessitated the reduction of one grade of the majority of the young officers in the army, he was demoted to the grade of First Lieutenant.

During the last three years, Captain Lee has made a host of friends among the faculty and students. He is the most popular member of the Military Faculty, and it has been said by some students that he is the most popular of all the faculty. His efficient and untiring ability as a leader in military, athletics, and other student activities has been demonstrated many times during this stay here.

Intramural and the regular college teams, especially in football, track and baseball have felt the results of his untiring ability. Also, much could be said about the way he has instilled the hard to define word, "College Spirit" into the student body.

The entrance to Camp Davis.

6

Panama

1926-29

Assignment to Panama seems to have caught Bill and Dava by surprise. It was fairly normal in the life of military officers that after a choice assignment such as ROTC, the next one would be more difficult. However, initially, Captain Lee was assigned to Tank School at Fort Meade; the orders were changed at the last minute.

Panama was one of four possible overseas postings along with China, the Philippines, and Hawaii. It really is unknown if Bill and Dava had any choice in the matter. Panama was considered one of the worst possible assignments and many were unsuited for it. With an equatorial climate, Panama became almost unbearable during the long rainy season, the threat of malaria constant. The mission of protecting the Canal was ambiguous at best. Captain Lee had already established himself as a top rate troubleshooter, and this could well have been one of the main reasons for his assignment.

Dava and Bill would miss their time in their hometown, at State, and in North Carolina—the good recreational times at the beach, the fishing, and hunting. But the pleasant trip by steamship through the South Atlantic, around the Florida Straits, and into the Gulf eased away their homesickness. As the sun began to shine warm upon their faces and the winds grew increasingly more gentle, Dava was very excited—this was her first trip abroad.

The assignment proved to be extremely challenging for Bill. Surprisingly, there were many recruits to be trained. He had not expected this, given the posture of the military. The expense of assigning young recruits immediately to overseas areas had been discontinued for the most part, or so Bill thought. However, using Captain Lee to turn raw recruits into first rate soldiers was a made-to-order assignment for this young professional. The high level of training of the soldiers in his company became one of his trademarks, along with his Saturday morning inspections.

Captain Lee worked especially hard at keeping his soldiers out of the more seamy side of Canal Zone duty by enlisting the support of the camp's doctors and chaplains. He made Saturday morning duty mandatory for his company, not so much because it was needed, but rather so he could keep track of his young, impressionable troops.

This was a time of flourishing for Dava also. As life for enlisted men was especially hard, Dava and Bill entertained often in their home. Dava became very close to many of the younger wives and seems to have taken at least one or two into her home when they were having difficulty. The Lees managed to find time for outdoor recreational activities and looked back on their time in the Canal Zone as extremely positive.

On the Way to Panama

By the time Bill and Dava reached Panama, they were ready for their new adventure. Bill wrote in a letter home that this assignment was going to be hard, but he was determined to make the best of it. At this stage, it is obvious that he has not completely decided to remain in the military.

At Home at Camp Davis

TOP:
Barracks housing the 14th Infantry

MIDDLE:
The Lees lived in the left half of this duplex.

BOTTOM:
The Lees' street.

OPPOSITE:
About halfway through their tour, the Lees moved into a roomier and airier home on the same street as their first duplex.

Ft.
Davis
1926-29

The 14th Infantry

Formation of the 14th Infantry.

The 14th Infantry at Camp Davis.

The monthly "pass in review." This was a competition drill and ceremony and Captain Lee's company won with great regularity.

Life Was Not All Duty

TOP:
Dava loved swimming and helped regularly in teaching military youngsters to swim.

MIDDLE, BOTTOM and OPPOSITE:
Bill and friends spent much free time on the water. He also learned to sail while in Panama.

The Tank School at Fort Meade, Maryland.

7
Back in the South
1929-32

The Lees returned to the Carolinas with hearts full of thankfulness. Neither had realized how much they would miss America—a feeling shared by most Americans with considerable time overseas. For Bill and his professional development, Panama had been a watershed. For one thing, it had shown him the need to make do with whatever one has. Panama had been the last link of the food chain; they received almost nothing—an infantry with few weapons and no ammunition and an artillery with no shells.

He was returning home to a different military in many ways, at least according to the readings he had done about the new machine gun and the use of planes in warfare, not to mention the bombing they could now do. It was going to be exciting.

After a few days visiting family and friends, Bill made his way to his new station at Fort Meade, Maryland to attend Tank School. He was already beginning to see armor as a tool that could turn the tide of battle. Along with fifty or so fellow students, Captain Lee began honing his skills in the use of battlefield armor. School duty was good—a reprieve from military routine. And, when Dava joined him, they took several trips to Virginia Beach and made wonderful friends among the students. Bill learned to play a decent game of chess and Dava became a formidable bridge partner.

TOP: Dava in front of their quarters. She liked Fort Meade with its rolling hills and picturesque views.

BOTTOM: When Bill and Dava moved to Fort Eustis, Virginia, Bill delighted in escorting family members on the "tour of the tanks."

Bill had shown such prowess in tactics that upon completion of the school, he was chosen to remain as the Commander of Tanks for demonstration purposes. This was a singular honor and a strong influence pointing his career toward tank warfare. What separated Bill Lee militarily from his fellow tacticians was that the enemy battlefield was always in his mind's eye. His responsibilities were enlarged when he moved down the peninsula to Fort Eustis as the operations officer for American Mechanized Forces, specifically to work on integrating ground troops with mechanized forces. It was also during this time that he made several trips to Washington and began developing the relationships which would eventually mean much to the airborne effort. Captain Lee was a tireless worker, and when he was selected to return to the Tank School as an instructor, it was a stroke of genius on the part of the decision makers. There seems to be indication that Dava and Bill became close friends of the George Pattons during this time. While the wives discussed their Red Cross volunteer activities or the Officers' Wives Club charity work, Bill and George engaged in endless hours of debate on battlefield tactics.

TOP:
Bill had a company of tanks to use for demonstration purposes for the Tank School. His interest in particular was to demonstrate maneuverability.

BELOW LEFT:
The Army was just learning about the possibilities of armor on the battlefield. Surprisingly, only a few in Captain Lee's class had actually been in World War I, where armor was used for the first time.

BELOW RIGHT:
Dava gets a look.

Time for recreation

Time out for a favorite activity. This was on the York River, Yorktown, Virginia.

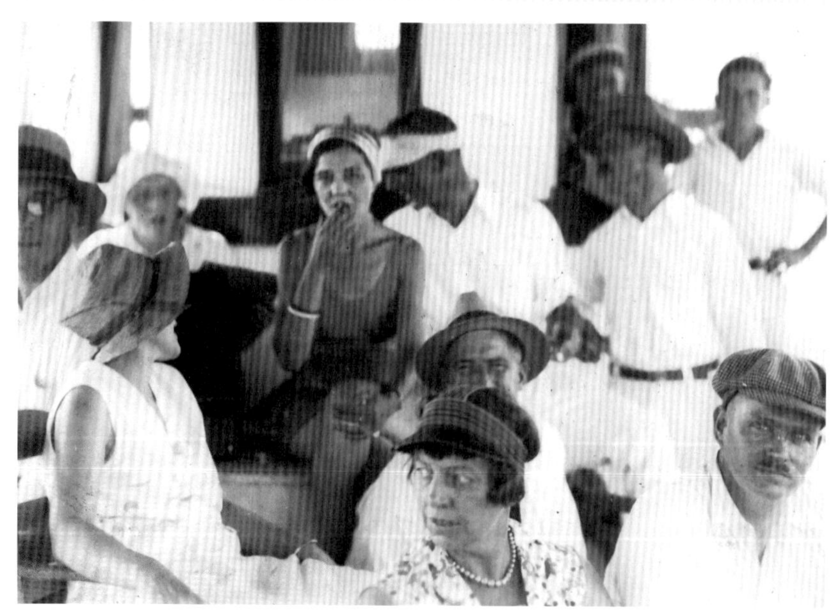

RIGHT:
Camping out at Virginia Beach.

BELOW:
Bill's favorite fishing spot was the Outer Banks of North Carolina.

Dunn, North Carolina

The South experienced unusual snowfall during the early thirties. On the back of one picture, Bill wrote, "Where was all of this when I was in high school?"

British maneuvers, 1932. Bill wrote in a letter that he bet Dava could not find him in the picture.

8
Observer in Europe
1932

America's Army had dwindled to a little over a hundred thousand and the isolationist mood still gripped the country when Bill and Dava traveled to Europe to observe the British tank maneuvers. The Maneuvers were a huge war game for practicing armor tactics—quite sophisticated for the day.

Dava settled in Paris, as they expected to spend three years abroad while Bill attended the French Tank School. They were delighted, but bliss was not to reign; Bill was soon notified that he had been selected to attend the Advance Infantry Course at Fort Benning. There is some evidence that he protested the move as not being cost effective but was told that his future was in tanks, and because of his knowledge, he should accept this as a natural progression in his career.

Captain Lee's experience with the Maneuvers became the genesis for his future position favoring British maneuverability over French tank intransigence. The British had built light tanks which could be maneuvered quickly, while the French Army in its mindset intended tanks to oppose from a static position somewhere to the rear of what they called the Maginot Line—hardened concrete fortifications constructed along the French and German border.

Bill traveled to Paris and Versailles, where he spent some time at the French tank school. He made friends with the American equivalent of the operations officer, a Lieutenant Yves Dumain, and they hit it off "famously." Mrs. Dumain and Dava became good friends, also, which gave Dava a chance to practice the French she had studied at the Greensboro College for Women.

Bill wrote beneath this picture, "The dear girl is a long way from Dunn."

British Maneuvers

The British soldier sitting on the front of the tank is a Corporal Dunmere. He and Bill became good friends, and upon their return to Europe, Bill and Dava visited with him on at least two occasions. When later General Lee returned to England for initial planning before America entered World War II, then-Sergeant Dunmere served as his personal liaison with the British Army.

France

Belleau Wood, France, 1932.

Bill loved his dog, Jere.

9
Infantry School
Fort Benning, Georgia, 1932-33

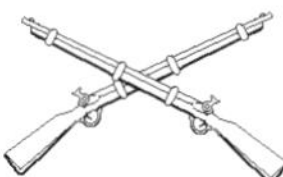

Bill and Dava's return to the States and to the Officer Advance Course must have seemed pretty anticlimactic after their whirlwind time in Europe.

The experience level among the officers in the course was quite varied. The mantle of the "old man" was pretty well accepted among Bill's peers—not in age, but in terms of experience. He was a natural leader—when he spoke, his classmates paid attention. He loved infantry tactics and often took various opposing sides just for the sake of debate. He was easily the most popular student in the course, and many of the instructors depended upon him to help with various lessons and military exercises.

For Dava, it was like returning home. She loved Fort Benning and seeing her friends, many assigned as instructors and others in the class with Bill. They lived in compact, cozy quarters on the post.

Fort Benning

Bill and Dava loved their house at Fort Benning. Dava often referred to it as their honeymoon cottage.

Time to relax

These were pleasant times for the Lees. Since they had time for leisure, Bill experimented with golf among other things.

10
Return to Europe

Student, French Tank School, Versailles, France, 1933-34
Staff Officer, French Army Tank Regiment, 1934
Office, Military Attaché, Paris & London, 1934-35

The Lees' return to Europe was to be a pivotal time in their military experience. Bill immediately began by participating in the British Maneuvers—the annual exercises of the British and French Armies. Since he had been involved with them in his previous short stint in Europe, this experience proved to be extremely meaningful and greatly enhanced his knowledge of armor on the battlefield and working with other armies.

The year's study at the French Tank School was fairly unregimented, but for Bill it meant learning an entirely new set of rules. He began in earnest his role as Dava's tour guide, and they traveled to almost all the places that he had visited after World War I.

After the student year came assignment to an actual French regiment. Bill served in all the levels of command from platoon leader to acting regimental commander. He had fun with it and learned the great possibilities of battlefield maneuver. The French, like his own countrymen, had the know-how to provide more and better equipment for training, but there was a vast difference between know-how and will. The French were willing to spend even less on armament than the United States, and Bill could not understand this as they were far more vulnerable to the whims of dictators and despots.

The British approach was different; they opted for small but well trained units. Bill discovered quickly that the military for many French officers was more social than actual. He abhorred this philosophy and frequent travel provided a good reason to be away from many of the social activities.

Dava became extremely popular with the French. One of her hobbies was to read French plays (in French) and then she and Bill would see them on stage. She also taught a very popular cooking class to the wives. One can only imagine the French learning to cook grits!

During the last year of his assignment, Bill became a liaison officer, traveling between Paris and London and visiting other armies of Europe. Always the student, the newly promoted Major Lee began to take close note of the aggressive military training of the German army and especially of men jumping from moving aircraft and of equipment and men being transported by glider. His intuitive mind immediately saw the possibilities of the Airborne—the idea of envelopment, what it could mean to an army in parachuting or landing behind enemy lines with ground soldiers and that even armor could be transported in planes. The seeds were sown and were to become his passion for the rest of his military career.

TOP:
The Lees return to Europe.

BOTTOM:
Bill's experience in the War continued to be a significant part of his memory as he and Dava visited this tribute to his old unit, the 3rd Division.

British Tank Maneuvers

With the French Army

LEFT:
Bill wrote beneath this picture: "An irrepressible, golden-hearted gentleman: Lieutenant Yves Dumain, Service des Affaires Indigènes. I knew him best as 'Speedy.' His joyous nature made a hard road easy."

RIGHT:
At the barracks in Angoulême.

BELOW LEFT:
Bill's company officers.

BELOW RIGHT:
Crews at French Tank School, Versailles.

The Lees' Travel Album
1933-35

The dapper Bill Lee from Dunn

On the road to Nazareth

Jerusalem

The pyramids and the Sphinx, Egypt

Alexandria

Off Sicily, Italy

On a canal in the Netherlands

Budapest, Hungary

Gibraltar

Frontier—Rhine River near Belfort

Oberammergau, Germany

Freiburg, Germany

The Acropolis, Athens

The Royal Palace, Athens

In the House of the Vestal Virgins

The site of the Colossus

The Square, St. Marks

Lisbon, Portugal

St. Peters, Rome

Coffee at St. Marks, Venice

Nice, France

Monte Carlo, France

Florence, Italy

Gibraltar

Location forgotten by Bill

Colosseum

Crossing the Channel

Major Lee and fellow instructors at the Infantry School.

11
Infantry School
Armor Force Tactics

Fort Benning, Georgia, 1935-37

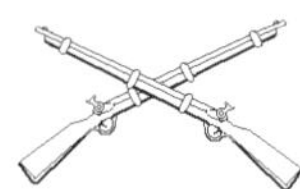

Major Lee's assignment to the Infantry School was a natural follow-up assignment to his time in Europe. He was now as close as one could be to being an expert in British and French armor. He had more than a working knowledge of the armor capabilities of most of the standing armies in existence. No one in the American army knew more about armor tactics than Bill Lee. George Patton was recognized as a great armor field leader, but at this particular time, Bill Lee was thought to have the edge over him in theory.

Coming back to Fort Benning was like returning to a second home. It was also a great classroom —a place for Bill to debate his views on the mobile battlefield, including the airborne. He did not abandon his idea of armor mobility, but it is also obvious that vertical envelopment, moving infantry by air, and the airborne were still germinating in his conscience. In fact, he produced a scholarly piece on the subject and submitted it to *Infantry Journal.*

Major Lee also served as a firsthand witness of many of the things he had seen overseas including German military training. When Hitler refused to shake the hand of Jessie Owens, winner of four gold medals in the Berlin Olympics of 1936, Bill Lee used the classroom to expound on Hitler's despotic views.

During this time Dava divided her time between Dunn, their hometown, and Fort Benning. The Lees began to think more and more toward retirement and buying a home or farm.

Bill participated in several tank maneuvers with the 66th Infantry. In fact, he was able to demonstrate both how the French and British used a combination of infantry and armor and the differences between the two.

Through a special arrangement with North Carolina State University, Bill completed the requirements for a degree in education. He did correspondence and traveled in his free time to Raleigh for classes and exams. His belief in the value of education was paramount and he entertained ideas of combining farming and teaching after retirement.

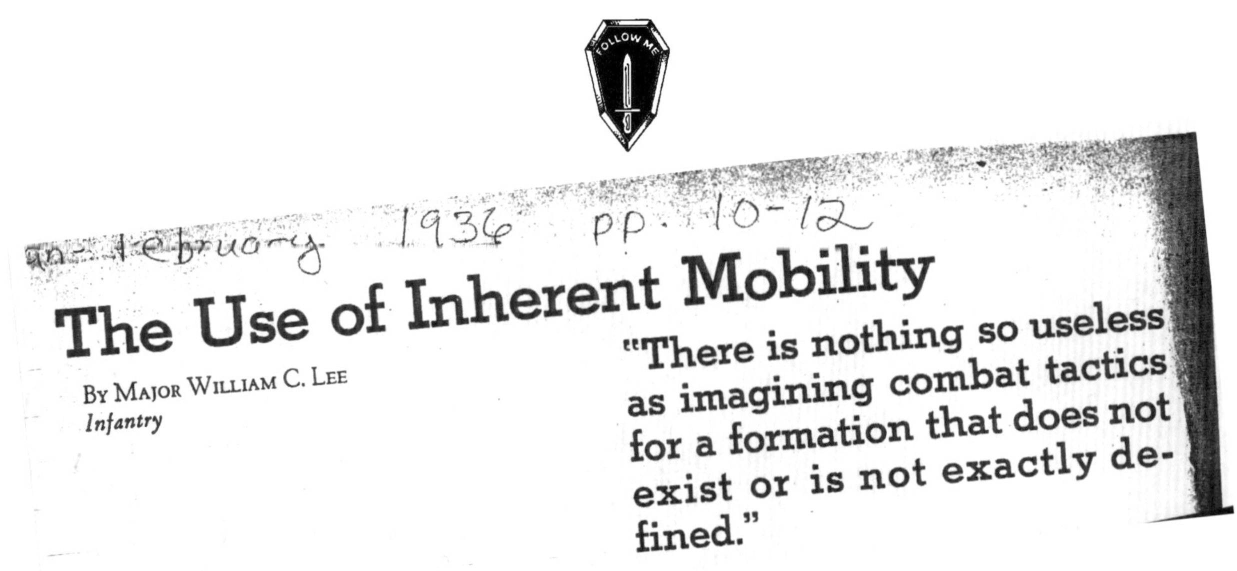

February 1936 pp. 10-12

The Use of Inherent Mobility

By Major William C. Lee
Infantry

"There is nothing so useless as imagining combat tactics for a formation that does not exist or is not exactly defined."

Bill demonstrated battlefield maneuverability with this tank company.

Leisure Time

It was not all work—Bill managed to engage in his favorite pastime.

18 Now At Benning Go To Leavenworth

Group Selected for Command and General Staff School.

WASHINGTON, Nov. 18.—The following Fort Benning officers have been assigned to Fort Leavenworth as students command and general staff school for the 1937-8 course:

Majors Lester N. Allyn, George S. Eyester, Frederick A. Irving, William C. Lee, Ronald L. Ring.

Captains Walter A. Bigby, Thomas J. Cross, Edwards S. Gibson, Laroy S. Graham, Joseph I. Greene, Edwin B. Howard, Robert G. Howie, Henry E. Kelly, Walter J. Muller, George C. Stewart, Robert N. Young, Edward J. Doyle, Charles A. Pyle.

Also Captain John F. Uncles, Columbus, now stationed at Schofield Barracks, T. H.

A SIGNAL HONOR

Officers of the army are not eligible to attend the War college until they have completed the course at the Leavenworth command and general staff school.

It is considered a signal honor in army circles for officers to be chosen for this course, because only those who have superior

Eighteen—Page 10—Col. 5

Bill Lee was chosen for Command and General Staff School.

12

Student, Command and General Staff School

Fort Leavenworth, Kansas, 1937-38

Fort Leavenworth, Kansas

Command and General Staff School was highly competitive and many of Major Lee's classmates would go on to achieve much in the military.

Bill Lee's selection to attend the year-long course at Command and General Staff School at Fort Leavenworth was an acknowledgment that he was moving to a higher level in his career. It seems to have caused Bill and Dava a certain amount of consternation, though. Accepting the assignment meant they were committed to several more years in the military, yet Bill enjoyed the land, had a farm, and in fact had been preparing to return home.

The Command and General Staff School had the reputation of testing the intellectual mettle of its students. The course prepared officers for battalion command and higher level staff positions. Like all military education, it was another rung in the advancement ladder. At times the course was lengthened to two years; at one time, as the war approached, it was shortened to six months. During the course, Bill made friendships and contacts with fellow students who would be running the military for years to come.

It was a good time for Dava and Bill as a couple. They lived in a big rambling multiplex apartment building on the north end of the post. Their place had high ceilings, wooden floors, and gorgeous marble cabinets. The building and every apartment had the charm of old world military. Dava decorated their place with a combination of pieces from their travels and local antiques she discovered.

The School and Fort Leavenworth meant new friends, trips into the Kansas countryside, and many moonlight walks on the old historic fort. Bill and Dava especially liked to take winter walks in the snow. As they huddled together when walking by the National Cemetery, one of the oldest in America, its beauty and sense of history gave them a great sense of pride in their decision to attend the course.

Amidst the academic challenges, and there were many, Bill tried out his ideas of vertical envelopment on his fellow classmates. His views in this academic lab met with much debate and also underwent some refinement. He became more and more convinced of the feasibility of his arguments. This was also a time of much discussion on what was happening in Europe and other strategic points around the globe. Bill Lee and most of his fellow students were convinced that going to war was merely a matter of time, and they were convinced that America could not have been less prepared.

Kansas Country

The surrounding Kansas countryside offered the Lees great opportunity to explore and enjoy the company of new friends. This particular outing was a picnic of Bill's school section.

Major Lee loved to be "out and about" as he called it. Here he is on an inspection tour of training with what few troops the brigade had.

13 Executive Officer, 1st Infantry Brigade

Oswego, New York, 1938-39

Bill's stint at Fort Leavenworth and Command and General Staff School had prepared him for an upper level higher headquarters staff job. When he and Dava settled in at Oswego, a distant outpost in upstate New York, they must have laughed at the idea that this was that higher level position. As the executive officer to the 1st Infantry Brigade, Bill could apply all the school solutions to whatever problems arose. The Brigade, however, was a far cry from being a textbook unit. Part of their mission was to help train the National Guard, and yet it was difficult to find enough people in their own unit to train. They were supposed to have three to five thousand troops, but five hundred on a good day was closer to reality. The Brigade was incredibly understaffed and completing even a minute task constituted a serious challenge.

Bill developed a training schedule as though they had a cast of thousands. The timing was perfect; they were perfectly positioned to take advantage of a presidential declaration of western hemisphere preparation. Although the country was not in immediate danger, an enemy could conceivably invade the shores of the U. S., and Major Lee took it upon himself to personally coordinate American and Canadian efforts to repel such an attack if it were ever to come.

Dava arranged trips to surrounding areas, and they especially enjoyed Niagara Falls. They traveled home often and continued to discuss retirement, but even the most casual observer of the world scene knew that something dire was looming on the horizon. Transatlantic flights had made the world smaller, but for most American citizens, the resolve to keep out of other countries' business remained the number one priority. In her heart, however, Dava believed that America would somehow find a way to go to war, and she knew that when that happened, her Bill would be right in the thick of it.

Dava Lee loved hats and had a different one for every occasion.

At Home

ABOVE:
Dava protested the quarters were much too big and they should go to some young family who had the children to fill up the house. Over the years it always amused her that the families with growing children were assigned "cracker box" houses and as they increased in rank and the children left home, the quarters were bigger.

BELOW:
Bill grew up at 111 West Divine Street, the house on the left. On September 30, 1935, the Lees purchased the home on the right, at 209 West Divine Street, Dunn.

Niagara Falls

Niagara Falls became a special place for the Lees. They visited the Falls several times and Dava referred to it as "many honeymoons."

Ocean Drive Beach

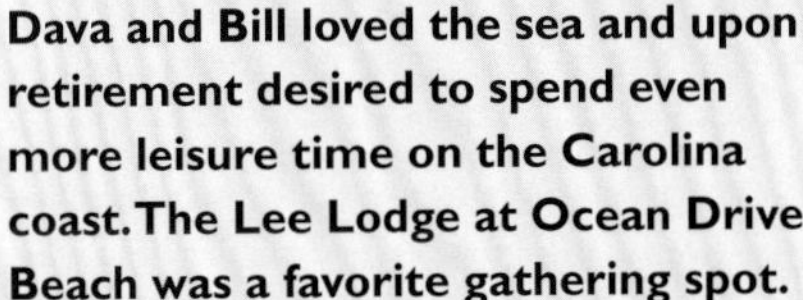

Dava and Bill loved the sea and upon retirement desired to spend even more leisure time on the Carolina coast. The Lee Lodge at Ocean Drive Beach was a favorite gathering spot.

Bill Lee the Farmer

TOP:
Bill Lee loved farming. Here he is with his cotton crew.

BELOW:
Dava sent him a picture of his new barn.

Bill wrote this letter to his brother Henry ...

I am glad that Eddie got his wheat in and that he has done as well as he has this year. I realize conditions under which he has had to operate and I am very pleased with the results that he got on Stoney Run farm and the Taylor Farm. I am delighted also that Dava has taken such an interest in the operation of the farms and that she is learning something about it. It not only gives her something to do, but gives her a feeling of doing something substantially and helpful to the war effort. I hope she keeps sufficient corn to carry through on our feeding projects for the coming year. In fact, it would be my idea to sell only the surplus corn now for which we have no housing facilities and to maintain a full barn until late because it can always be sold if we don't need it. However, whatever she does will be quite satisfactory to me.

From the Chief's Office

Commissioned Personnel, Office Chief of Infantry

Chief of Infantry
MAJOR GENERAL GEORGE A. LYNCH

Executive
COLONEL EUGENE W. FALES

Personnel Section
COLONEL MAXON S. LOUGH
LIEUTENANT COLONEL NORMAN RANDOLPH
LIEUTENANT COLONEL HENRY J. MATCHETT
MAJOR WILLIAM B. KEAN
FIRST LIEUTENANT HOLMAN D. HOOVER

Arms, Equipment, and Finance Section
LIEUTENANT COLONEL WILLIAM F. LEE
LIEUTENANT COLONEL GRANT A. SCHLIEKER
LIEUTENANT COLONEL INGOMAR M. OSETH
LIEUTENANT COLONEL WALTER G. LAYMAN

Training Section
LIEUTENANT COLONEL PAUL J. MUELLER
LIEUTENANT COLONEL JAMES W. CURTIS
LIEUTENANT COLONEL WILLIAM C. LEE
LIEUTENANT COLONEL EDWARD H. CONNOR, JR.
MAJOR JOSEPH I. GREENE
MAJOR WENDELL G. JOHNSON
CAPTAIN RIDGELY GAITHER, JR.
CAPTAIN J. R. ULMER
FIRST LIEUTENANT W. H. MCELDOWNEY

Intelligence Section
MAJOR ALBERT C. WEDEMEYER
CAPTAIN CARL T. SCHMIDT

Air Infantry

By Lieutenant Colonel William C. Lee, Infantry

Nowadays two kinds of infantry ride in airplanes, and there is a distinct difference between them—air

land. Hence it is the business of parachute infantry t[illegible] capture airfields—as these troops did in Holland. In th[illegible] Low Countries wide stretches of paved roads were als[illegible]

14

The Airborne Project

Detailed to War Department, 1939
Airborne Project Assigned, 1940
Provisional Parachute Group, 1941-42

Bill Lee's assignment to the Chief of Infantry's office is shrouded somewhat in mystery. George Lynch, the venerable two-star general and Chief of the Department, was looking for a tanker. However, the "comers" at the War Department who were usually tapped weren't eager to transfer to the Chief. Much of what the Chief of Infantry did on various studies and projects was considered routine work, and those assigned to Infantry were much less likely to get noticed for a future assignment. George Lynch was known as a hard task master and somewhat anachronistic.

Someone at the War Department, possibly General Mark Clark himself, suggested Major W. C. Lee. It could have been General Marshall. There is some evidence that Marshall knew Lee in World War I and was aware that they had both been in the Sigma Nu fraternity—Lee at North Carolina State and Marshall at Virginia Military Institute. General Lynch immediately arranged for an interview. Bill was accepted and the Lees moved to Camp Humphreys, now Fort Belvoir, just outside Washington. There is some speculation that Marshall may have been frustrated by the fractious infighting concerning the airborne concept and knew of Lee's keen interest in it. Documentation existed of German and Russian use of airborne troops and air landing, and on at least three occasions, questions had been raised about the need and feasibility of such a force. Of course, the earliest mention of the possibility of parachuting from a plane was by maverick General Billy Mitchell in 1918. Lee was assigned to the training section in the Chief of Infantry office and did several creditable pieces of work relating to armor before he authored a study on the feasibility of air infantry. But this study, along with other work on the airborne, was shelved—primarily because of the priority of other projects. Major Lee was incredulous that Axis powers had mastered airborne, yet his own military had no initiative to move on it.

Bill Lee loved these words of Abraham Lincoln: "I will prepare myself and when the time is right, I will be ready."

The resurrection of the airborne is one of those mythical stories in which truth is definitely stranger than fiction. Major Lee's enthusiasm for the entire paratrooper concept had gotten under his immediate supervisor's skin. Lee had been hired to coordinate armor efforts and to be the resident expert on foreign armor, and the Colonel wanted him to stick to his assigned task—no more talk of the airborne. But according to the story, President Franklin Delano Roosevelt was watching newsreels in his Hyde Park home and saw German paratroopers leaping from airplanes. The President immediately summoned Pa Watson, his military liaison, to find out about America's own paratrooper capability.

The rest is history.

OPPOSITE:
Lee had a great appreciation for the pilots of the Air Corps and felt they were often the unsung heroes of the airborne. He is shown in front of an AT (advanced trainer) which often ferried him on his frequent trips from Washington to Lawson Field.

The Airborne Project

Major Bill Lee was officially assigned the airborne project on June 25, 1940. It was prophetic that, on the same day, the French were surrendering to the Germans in a railroad car in which they had received the German surrender in 1918. The isolationist mood still existed in America even as FDR sought to pull the rest of the country into the reality of a coming war. Poland was history already and the President used its fall to declare a limited national emergency that authorized 17,000 regular troops, 6000 aircraft, and 50,000 men. This move was absolutely critical to the airborne effort-no planes, no airborne.

World events further delivered the goods. The faked German inactivity had lulled many Americans, but they quickly awakened when the vast German industrial machine, including extremely effective use of airborne troops, moved into France and Belgium.

In May, the President asked Congress for 50,000 planes and money to prepare America for what many knew to be inevitable. Bill Lee wasted no time. The airborne project had been under way in his own mind for at least five years. When this charming and subtle Southerner arrived at the Air Corps headquarters pleading his case, he was surprisingly well received and left with his want list filled. He had coordinated extensively with Fort Benning's Infantry School and had given them a "heads up" on the possibilities. Miraculously, in less than three weeks, the charismatic Major had everything he needed, and the bold experiment began with a carefully chosen test platoon. Major Lee had no doubt that it would work; he had already seen the prowess of German paratroopers, and using his vast network of contacts, mostly from overseas sources, he had secured a standard operating procedure manual of the German airborne.

Major Lee was a man possessed as he moved to get his airborne established and ready, but it was no picnic. He wrote later on ...

> *I did meet with many obstacles sometimes seemingly impossible to overcome, but they were obstacles caused by conditions rather than men....the army was tragically short of everything. Tremendous expansion was under way in all arms and branches. Industry had hardly started to convert to production of munitions and vital equipment. Everybody wanted everything, all at once, and it just couldn't be had. Every field commander considered his particular project or command the most important thing in the army, and if he was worth his salt he was fighting like a tiger for funds and equipment. Harassed and overworked staff officers in Washington had innumerable decisions to make every day as to where to send what little stuff was available. By force of circumstances, they had to favor one project and deny another. There simply wasn't enough stuff to go around. It was a matter of 2 and 2 being 4 and not 400.*

PARACHUTE TEST PLATOON
1st Row: Haley, Kelly, Smith, Ward, Kitchens, Ivy, Poudert, Peters, McLaney, Coley, Montisett, Shepherd
2nd Row: Corbin, Burkhalter, Roberts, Brown, King, Rutland, Hardin, McCullough, Kasell, Dodd, Willson
3rd Row: Voils, Builbeau, Pitts, Doucet, Lt. Rider, Lt. Bassett, W/O Wilson, Wallace, Harris, Wade, Pursley, Davis, Skipper
4th Row: Resse, Robinson, Jacquay, Cornellious, Selman, Kirksey, Eberhardt, Weeks, Borom, Adams, Tracy
Absent: Brown, L., Dilburn, Ellis, Houston, Ketcherside, Swilley, Willson, O., Yates

The creation of the test platoon was a drama rivaling any in the annals of military history. Almost all airborne tradition evolved from the work of these courageous, unorthodox pioneers. This history-making group of patriots was established on July 1, 1940. Witnessing their beginning was like watching a great stage play—one drama after another. Exploring the history of the platoon is a must for even the casually interested.

Paratroopers are volunteers.

The drama of the Airborne began in darkness as leaders announced to their assembled charges the formation of a voluntary test platoon—despite the unwritten rule in the army of 1940 that "nobody volunteers."

There was a sobering list of requirements: a minimum of two years infantry service, weight no more than 185 pounds, unmarried, excellent physical condition. The volunteer would be required to make frequent jumps from airplanes in flight at various altitudes, which could result in serious injury or death.

More than two hundred men accepted the challenge.

Parachute Provisional Group, Fort Benning, Georgia, 1941-42

World events were moving rapidly, as was the growing airborne movement. Flush with the success of the test platoon, the 501st battalion was born on October 1,1940. Its mission was to train and provide cadre for the ever-expanding airborne. Shortages were much a part of life but Bill Lee, the innovative and creative project officer, kept things moving. Intense training and accomplishment—and the idea that these men had done what others hadn't—produced a type of bravado in the battalion that was difficult to keep in check. Special insignia came into being, along with various badges of courage, the swagger and all the extraneous paraphernalia that goes with being elite.

The morale of an accomplished paratrooper was far superior to that of the regular trooper. Superior leadership and a stable hand were needed to save the airborne from itself. Consequently, Bill Lee, less than six months a Lieutenant Colonel, became the commander of the newly formed Parachute Provisional Group.

The Group was to take charge of training, organize the jump school, and get the Army ready for an expanded airborne ready to go to war. A mountain of administrative obstacles confronted Lieutenant Colonel Lee—shortages of equipment, the makeup and design of the units, and sticky turf issues with the post. Few men in the Army would have had diplomatic skills equal to the task. Lee's leadership style, based on the Biblical principle of Micah 6:8 ("do justly, love mercy, and walk humbly with thy God"), which he kept open on his desk, provided a steadying influence for those early airborne growing pains.

officer, Tilton General Hospital, for duty. The travel directed is necessary in the military service. FD 1416 P 1-0620, 80-0600 A 0410-01. (A. G. 210.31.) (19 Feb. 41.)

11. Lieutenant Colonel *William C. Lee* (O-8381), Infantry, is relieved from assignment and duty in the office of the Chief of Infantry, Washington, D. C., effective on or about 31 March, 1941, is then assigned to the Provisional Parachute Group, Fort Benning, Georgia, and will proceed to that station and report for duty. The travel directed is necessary in the military service. FD 1408 P 1-0620, 80-0600 A 0410-01. If the travel is performed by privately owned automobile detached service for three days is authorized.

12. Lieutenant Colonel *John C. Green* (O-10201), Signal Corps, is relieved from assignment and duty with the Thirty-seventh Division, Camp Shelby, Mississippi, effective on or about 1 June, 1941, is then assigned to the 63d Signal Battalion, Camp Claiborne, Louisiana, and will proceed to that station and report for duty.

Bill recognized the prima donna persona and allowed the men their swagger while keeping them rooted in reality. He, more than most, realized that it was that paratrooper swagger, that belief in the transcendence of the paratrooper, that would one day lead them to jump from a moving aircraft, hit the ground fighting, tackle impossible enemy odds; this feeling of invulnerability would keep them alive.

"We wanted them cocky, self confident, even to the point of conceit; aggressive; and above all, proud; but we insisted on good discipline."

OPPOSITE:
Lieutenant Colonel William C. Lee, commander of the Provisional Parachute Group on the drop zone at Fort Benning , after his first parachute jump. The rapid expansion of the airborne had already produced the 501st battalion, with the 502nd, 503rd, and 504th just around the corner. Later the 88th would be formed to test and experiment with operational procedures. Each battalion was to number 36 officers and 483 enlisted men. The call for recruits yielded almost no response until Lieutenant Colonel Lee took matters into his own hands, and journeyed to Fort Bragg to talk with the 9th Infantry. He needed at least 172 potential paratroopers initially. Over 1000 volunteered.

TALK TO OFFICERS OF PROVISIONAL PARACHUTE GROUP
By
Lieutenant Colonel William C. Lee
October 4, 1941.

I realize the inconvenience of calling an officers' meeting such as this, but such meetings are necessary occasionally in order that we may take stock of ourselves and our progress and indicate anew our objectives and our aims. I think it is only fair that you should be told what we expect of you in order that you may guide yourselves accordingly....

STANDARDS. We are very proud of the high standards reached by our officers in appearance, conduct, and efficiency. We like to think of ourselves as a corps d'élite, and we are. I suspect that we are the envy of the Army in many respects. I have no doubt that each of us is prouder of our organization than we have ever been of any other. The insignia we wear on our caps sets us apart and we wear it with a peculiar pride. All over the country, wherever we go, our uniform and our markings immediately attract the attention of all, and we are, in the words of the British Major Martin, autographed, photographed, stared at and admired.

Needless to say, we strut, and we are proud to strut, and I want you to continue to strut with head high and with chest out. As long as we have pride of organization and a high spirit, we need never worry about morale in our outfit. Men who daily share a common danger, and whose courage is tried and found not wanting, feel closer to each other than does the common run of soldier, and down in our hearts we not only respect our men and our fellow officers, but we know that in time of desperate need, our confidence in each other will not fail.

The newspapers speak of us as the glamour boys of the Army. We have had a great deal of favorable publicity—I'm afraid too much. But I assure you that jumping from an airplane is not alone going to keep us in this high place before the public eye. I especially want to warn you about this. Our daily conduct on duty and off, our personal appearance, our industry and application to our work—they are the things which count most. Only by our efficiency, our honor, our conduct and our integrity can we be really worthy of the respect of our men, of the Army as a whole, and of the civilian public.

We must require certain standards of our officers, and those standards are high. I have no doubt that you will continue to live up to them, but should you consistently show that you cannot or will not, then your release from this unit will be swift and sure....

As a final word, I want to say that we strive for perfection even though we may not obtain it. We will all make our mistakes but don't be discouraged by mistakes. We will learn from experience. If we are right fifty percent of the time, we are batting 500 and that's a damn good average in any man's league.

HEADQUARTERS
Provisional Parachute Group
Fort Benning, Georgia
February 28, 1942

To the Officers & Men:

We are now at war. Today we are faced with the task of building up a well trained parachute force which, when called upon for the inevitable test of its ability as a fighting unit in combat with the enemy, will efficiently and relentlessly carry out its mission to its complete success.

To this end we must devote all our time and energy. This will demand of each officer and enlisted man now members of the Parachute Group, and those to come to us in the future, hard work, long hours, initiative, and attention to duty never before required. The dividends will be paid on the battlefield.

I know, and you know, that we have the courage. Loyalty, character, high morale, spirit of comradeship, enthusiasm, and the will to win has always been evident in this, the finest command in the United States Army. However, that is not quite enough to win. When the crucial moment comes and the commands "Hook Up" and "Stand to Door" are given, let us be completely trained for the task to be performed. Victory then will be inevitable.

W.C. Lee.

Bill Lee was a constant cheerleader for his paratroopers. He pushed and pushed and experimented. Jim Gavin, Lee's Operations Officer and a man who was to go on to great fame, said of those days, "Lieutenant Colonel Lee was a smart, patient, tolerant, considerate, intelligent, and kind man. He struggled with us—we kids wanted to rebuild the world right away. There were all sorts of things we were wild-eyed about and having a great old time doing. Jumping every place under the sun. He let us try anything we wanted to do. And we did. But he applied a governing hand—and good common sense. There couldn't have been a better man for the job."

The plane roared down the runway, and just when it seemed that it was never going to get off the ground, I could see the tops of the trees and in the distance the outline of the ground and sky. It was straining, climbing higher and higher. My heart was racing and I was trying to remain calm. My mouth was dry and I tried to think of other things. For a long time, the idea of jumping myself had not even entered my mind. Throughout the training of the test platoon, as I studied German airborne operations, and then as the 501st moved into high gear, I knew this day would come.

Dava thought I was crazy. Why do you have to do it? She knew the answer and also knew it was futile to talk about it. Jumping out of an airplane at 1500 to 3000 feet in the sky was not a joy ride or the state fair. People were killed and injured, and in her heart she didn't see any need for it. But in her being, she knew I would do it.

THOSE SILVER WINGS. **Bill Lee was 47 years old when he made his first parachute jump. Time did not permit him to receive full training, but he worked with his charges to develop a course of study that consisted of six weeks of training, including 56 hours of education in parachute packing, 40 hours in training on the harness apparatus, and 32 hours on the jump towers. To qualify for the silver wings, troopers had to make five jumps, and two must be simulated mass combat jumps of no less than 12 men. At various times, based on the mission, different aspects of the training have varied slightly, but over the long haul, even today it remains the same.**

How in the world could I be involved in asking men to risk their own lives when I had not parachuted from a moving plane myself? I needed to experience every aspect of it before I could possibly talk authoritatively about it. I constantly told myself this was all a means to an end. The jumping out of airplanes was not the epiphany, it was transportation to the fight. But, there was something about it which tested the mettle of the man, that which made him what he was, to be able to, in fact, wage battle. It was not for everybody and that was why it was strictly voluntary.

A commander needs to be a part of the experience and shouldn't even be chosen for the awesome job of leading paratroopers if he has not himself been tested in the art of the craft. Thanks to Tug, I feel I've had good training. Hooking up the static line running from the casing of the parachute to the cable that ran from front to back meant no turning back. I lowered my head and followed the trooper in front of me out the door—a hard body position, tucked in arms, grabbed the reserve, started counting—thousand one, thousand two. Suddenly I felt the pop of the chute and it was open. And that glorious float started—THANK YOU LORD. The ground was coming up fast and I braced myself, prepared to initiate a good landing—relax, roll. I was on my feet before I knew it. All the practice paid off.

Dava's favorite photo. Notice the airborne patch on the left of the hat. The early airborne pioneers were incredibly creative. Colonel Lee thought the badges and the patches added to morale, but he often did not wear them.

15

Airborne Command

March 22, 1942

Bill Lee was working 16 to 18 hours a day in the Provisional Parachute Group. With the call for more and more training and experimenting, shortages of everything, even including parachutes, the administrative and logistical problems numbered in the thousands. Added to this were the many disciplinary problems, mostly brought about by combinations of circumstances and people, not the least innocent of which were the rambunctious paratroopers themselves, who trained and played hard.

A complicating problem was the level of authority that the post—the "legs"—had over the men. Most of the time, the Provisional Paratrooper Command could only serve as a big brother, and Lee's diplomatic skills often saved the embryonic airborne from disaster. Lee also had to fight strong opinion from the War Department that the airborne was consuming too many resources and that the nation would best be served by developing traditional leg infantry divisions and conserving resources.

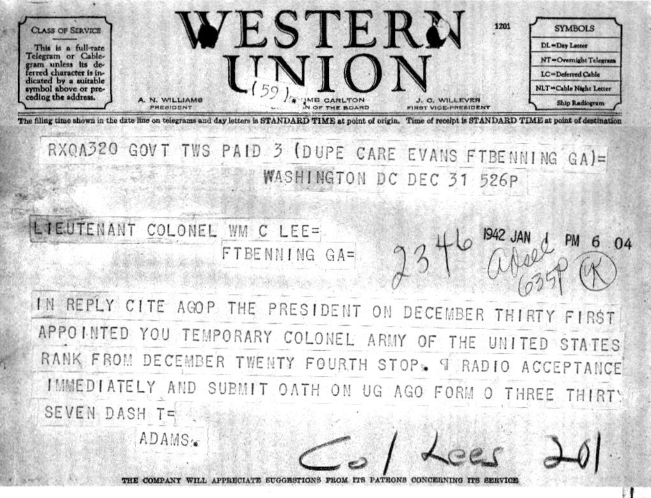
WESTERN UNION

RXQA320 GOVT TWS PAID 3 (DUPE CARE EVANS FTBENNING GA)= WASHINGTON DC DEC 31 526P

LIEUTENANT COLONEL WM C LEE=
FTBENNING GA=

IN REPLY CITE AGOP THE PRESIDENT ON DECEMBER THIRTY FIRST APPOINTED YOU TEMPORARY COLONEL ARMY OF THE UNITED STATES RANK FROM DECEMBER TWENTY FOURTH STOP. RADIO ACCEPTANCE IMMEDIATELY AND SUBMIT OATH ON UG AGO FORM O THREE THIRTY SEVEN DASH T=
ADAMS.

Col Lees 201

The airborne capture of the island of Crete with 13,000 paratroopers gave new leverage to Lee's advocacy of independent airborne fighting forces. Fighting bureaucracy and colossal shortages were bad enough, but the crowning blow was competition for training areas at Fort Benning's sprawling 97,000 acres. The two principle players at Fort Benning—Lee's Airborne and George Patton's tanks—both required vast amounts of space. Lee convinced the War Department after successful maneuvers in Panama that additional training areas were needed, and at his request, a gigantic tract of land was purchased across the Chattahoochee River in Alabama to be used strictly by airborne forces.

A few days after Pearl Harbor, Lieutenant Colonel Lee became Colonel Lee and was in effect a regimental commander with all parachute battalions under his command. Army Ground Forces, a new Command, responsible for the creation of 100 American fighting divisions, was also born. Lee understood immediately that he must make a bold move to establish the Airborne as a separate command lest it be swallowed up in this new configuration.

He traveled to Washington to convince Army Ground Forces of the need for all airborne operations to be under one command and to lobby for a new home for the Airborne. His suggestion was Fort Bragg, North Carolina. Space existed at the large military post in the sandhills and it was ideally suited for airborne operations because of adjacent airfields and friendly terrain. Consequently, Airborne Command was established directly under AGF and its new home became Fort Bragg, North Carolina. The fact that it was close to Colonel Lee's hometown was of no small significance in his choice. He never denied this fact nor that the Airborne was the symbol of American preparation for the coming war.

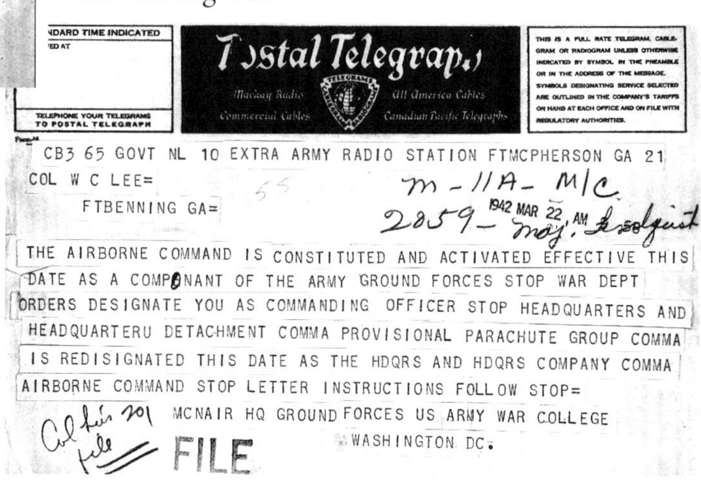
Postal Telegraph

CB3 65 GOVT NL 10 EXTRA ARMY RADIO STATION FTMCPHERSON GA 21
COL W C LEE=
FTBENNING GA=

THE AIRBORNE COMMAND IS CONSTITUTED AND ACTIVATED EFFECTIVE THIS DATE AS A COMPONANT OF THE ARMY GROUND FORCES STOP WAR DEPT ORDERS DESIGNATE YOU AS COMMANDING OFFICER STOP HEADQUARTERS AND HEADQUARTERU DETACHMENT COMMA PROVISIONAL PARACHUTE GROUP COMMA IS REDISIGNATED THIS DATE AS THE HDQRS AND HDQRS COMPANY COMMA AIRBORNE COMMAND STOP LETTER INSTRUCTIONS FOLLOW STOP=
MCNAIR HQ GROUND FORCES US ARMY WAR COLLEGE
WASHINGTON DC.

FILE

When Colonel Lee received his mission orders from Lieutenant General Lesley J. "Whitey" McNair, of Army Ground Forces, a lesser individual would have seen it as a "Mission Impossible" scenario—to organize and train special airborne ground units, such as parachute, air-landing infantry and artillery; continue airborne training of such other ground force units; control allocation and training of such Air Corps transport airplane or glider units as may be available by Army Air Forces; coordinate training with Army Air Force combat units; determine operating procedures for airborne operations and supply of large forces; and, in coordination with the Navy, determine procedures for joint airborne-seaborne operations.

Colonel Lee Activates the 502d and 503d Parachute Regiments

ADDRESS
Of
Colonel William C. Lee, Commanding Officer
of The Provisional Parachute Group, at Activation Ceremony
of the 502d and 503d Parachute Regiments,
Fort Benning, Georgia,
March 7, 1942.

Officers and men of the 503d and 502d Parachute Regiments, this is a memorable day for American Parachute Troops. You are grouped for the first time into regiments. We shall not forget the 501st, the 502d, and the 504th Parachute Battalions, for those units were the pioneers; the ones which made these regiments possible. Today those units exist no more as separate battalions. Instead you have a larger and more powerful unit; one which increases your fighting and staying power; and one which magnifies your chances of success in battle.

During these past two weeks of reorganization there have been discomforts and confusion due to inevitable changes and shifting of personnel. I know that you have understood those conditions. I know also that you have accepted them with fortitude and without complaint. Not everyone can have the assignment to the unit of his choice, but being soldiers, and ABOVE ALL PARACHUTISTS, we go where we can serve best. I ask each of you to take with you into your regiments the same loyalty, esprit, and discipline that made your old battalions famous.

Among men of proven courage, such as you, there is a bond of comradeship and mutual respect which differences in rank cannot efface. May that mutual respect and comradeship be the abiding influence which, in the days to come, will bring fame to these regiments and honor to yourselves. May the presentation of these Colors today kindle ever higher our devotion to our country and inspire in each of us a grim determination to endure the hardships of the future, PROUD and UNAFRAID. This is the spirit which in the end will bring us victory.

I congratulate Colonel Miley and Colonel Howell on having the finest commands in the United States Army; and I congratulate the rest of you on having two such fine and able officers as your commanders. You may rest assured that your welfare will always be uppermost in their minds.

OPPOSITE:
Colonel Lee with two of his protégés. Bud Miley, on his right, was the commander of the first airborne battalion in the Army. He was hand-picked by Lee and went on eventually to command the 17th Airborne Division. To Colonel Lee's left is George P. Howell, at that time the Commandant of the Parachute School. The Airborne School trained over 100,000 paratroopers in four years.

Mark Clark was one of Bill Lee's strongest supporters at the War Department in early airborne days. Clark said of Lee's paratroopers, "I, for one, feel that these units should be expanded materially, for they are mighty handy to have around when a difficult job is to be done."

OPPOSITE:

"...The Airborne Command consisted of a headquarters, the Parachute School, two parachute regiments, the 88th Airborne Bn, a test parachute artillery battery, and two or three other small test or experimental units. Plans were under way for the activation of a number of additional parachute regiments and some experimental glider outfits. No definite plans had been made for the activation of airborne divisions, the idea of the General Staff at the time being that ordinary infantry divisions would be trained for airborne work. I had proposed the organization of airborne divisions a year or two earlier and had been harping on that idea since early 1940, but had not been able to finally sell it to the General Staff."

EXEC O

Mrs D —
Personal File WCL

201 — Lee

WCL:cd

June 11, 1942

Captain Harry Wilson
Parachute School
Fort Benning, Georgia

Dear Tug:

I returned to Fort Bragg last night. One of the first matters that Colonel Chapman took up with me was your request for a transfer from the Airborne Command. Only for one reason will I approve your request and that is if you have definite assurance that you can improve yourself or secure advancement faster than I can give it to you. I will not stand in your way. But on the other hand, the time has arrived when personalities can no longer be considered. Each one of us must fit into the job for which we are best suited and pitch for all we are worth without thought of self in any respect.

I need you and need you badly in our work and it would be a severe loss to me should you leave us at this time. Big things are brewing and I have your work cut out for you. Therefore, your application for transfer has been suspended at this office until I can see and talk with you. I will be at Fort Benning next week. With best wishes to Mrs. Wilson and yourself, I am

Sincerely yours,

WILLIAM C. LEE,
Brigadier General, U. S. A.,
Commanding.

Columbia, South Carolina, June 27, 1942. Equipped with a ground unit of a plane-to-field radio, Prime Minister Winston Churchill closes his eyes to better hear the orders being given paratroopers he reviewed on a surprise visit to Fort Jackson.

1WVR Y 27 WD

WASHN DC 621P APR 16 1942

COL WILLIAM C LEE

INF PROVISIONAL PARACHUTE GROUP FTBENNING GA

THE PRESIDENT HAS SUBMITTED TO SENATE NOMINATION FOR YOUR APPOINTMENT AS BRIGADIER GENERAL AUS STOP RADIO ACCEPTANCE STATING ACCEPTANCE EFFECTIVE AS OF APPOINTMENT DATE END SPXOP

ULIO

110A APR 17-

STANDARD FORM No. 14A
APPROVED BY THE PRESIDENT
MARCH 10, 1926

TELEGRAM

OFFICIAL BUSINESS—GOVERNMENT RATES

FROM: WAR DEPARTMENT
I certify that this telegram is
BUREAU official business and
necessary in the public service.

THORNTON CHASE
Colonel, AGD, Adjt. Gen.

THE ADJUTANT GENERAL
WASHINGTON DC

I HEREBY ACCEPT APPOINTMENT AS BRIGADIER GENERAL AUS EFFECTIVE AS OF APPOINTMENT DATE.

WILLIAM C. LEE

16
Victory Day in Dunn

June 11, 1942

Hon. J. N. Creel, Mayor
Dunn, North Carolina

Dear Joe:

I have been away for some time and have just returned to Fort Bragg where I found your letter of May 15. I feel very humble and grateful for your plans to include me in the program for your 4-day victory celebration. I do not consider myself in any way entitled to the honor which you propose to do me and if I had my way about it, I would suggest that the "General Lee" part of the program be eliminated. I think that my home folks have exaggerated my rank, my job, and my importance ,out of all proportion to what it should be.

On the other hand, in view of the fact that it is your opinion that my presence might add in some way to the success of your celebration, I cannot bring myself to refuse to accept this great honor. If the celebration were to be held at any place other than in my home town and by my own folks, I would not think of accepting it. So if the military situation permits, I will plan to be present at Dunn on July 3 or at least a part of the day.

I would personally prefer that the honor which you propose to confer on me be suspended until after it was earned but since you have already made your plans, I assure you that I will do everything that I can to contribute to the success of the victory celebration. I am unable to express the deep appreciation I feel towards the people of Dunn for thinking of me

July 8, 1942

Honorable Joe Creel, Mayor,
Dunn, North Carolina.

My dear Joe:

This is to try to express my appreciation for all of the nice things you did for me last Friday. The luncheon which you gave was especially nice, the program was attractive, and the food was good. I am writing a more or less formal letter to you,as Mayor, and to the Board of Commissioners. This letter will be mailed in a few days.

I believe the day was the most pleasant one of my life and I hope in some way you will permit me to try to return your hospitality. Will be seeing you soon.

Sincerely,

WILLIAM C. LEE,
Brigadier General, U. S. A.,
Commanding.

The Reluctant General Is Feted

RIGHT:
General Lee watches the parade with Governor Broughton.

Army Chief of Staff George C. Marshall inspects the troops.

17
First Trip to England

1942

After reviewing the capabilities of the airborne troops in North Carolina, General Marshall was convinced that the Airborne would play a vital role in subduing Hitler's army in Europe. He ordered General Lee to England to begin the planning of the Cross-Channel invasion. General Lee recounts:

"About the middle of May, I received a telephone call one night from General Mark Clark, Chief of Staff, AGF, to come to Washington next morning prepared for an overseas trip. On arrival at AGF next day, General Clark informed me that I was going to London with a party consisting of himself, General Eisenhower, General Somervell, General Arnold, and one or two others. I went in General Somervell's plane, arriving in London sometime after May 15th, where I joined the rest of the party.

"On my arrival General Clark informed me of a proposed invasion of the continent at some future date and directed that I study the general plans developed up to that point, to consult with British airborne commanders, to visit and study British airborne installations, and on return to this country be prepared to recommend airborne needs for the proposed invasion of France. All this I did, studying in particular the general outlines of the invasion plan ... it was to take place in late spring or early summer of 1943. Definite landing places in France had not been selected, of course, as the combined Chiefs of Staff had not at this time approved a precise plan. However, the Cherbourg Peninsula was looked upon as a very possible landing place along with the beaches and coast to the east of Cherbourg. The area around Le Havre was also being considered.

"The planners at that time were considering using only two American Parachute regiments along with the one British Airborne Division. In general, the British Airborne Forces were to support the British effort and American parachute units were to support the American effort. Even at that time there was to be a clear division between the American and British Forces. However, General F. A. M. Browning, British Airborne Commander, was urging the formation of a combined British-American Airborne Force under one command to be used in either the British or American sectors, or both, depending on available air transport.

"While in London, I immediately called the planner's attention to the fact that two American Parachute regiments would be utterly inadequate to accomplish the airborne mission and that we would need many more airborne troops. I was told by General Clark to make a complete study of our needs and to be prepared to submit recommendations immediately on my return to Washington.

"I considered the British Airborne Division to be the proper approach to the problem of organizing for our airborne forces, with additional parachute infantry brigades for special missions. However, I didn't like the British Airborne Division organization. I thought it was too heavy and cumbersome, and a lighter division was indicated for the American forces.

"On return to Washington, I recommended to General Clark that we should organize airborne divisions of about 10 or 12 thousand men each and separate parachute infantry brigades of about 4500 men each, each brigade to be reinforced with artillery and special units.

"I especially recommended that one American Airborne Division and one American parachute brigade be organized, equipped and trained as soon as possible for the 1943 operation. These recommendations were approved by General Clark."

The Commander Inspects the Troops

Commanding Chief of Staff of the Army, George C. Marshall, looking over airborne troops at Pope Field, Fort Bragg. With him is Field Marshal Sir John Dill, the senior British officer on duty in Washington. Brigadier General Lee is credited with much of the success of close relations between many American and British officers at the command level, especially among the airborne forces. His easy-going nature, ability to listen, and impeccable manners were often cited by his British counterparts.

Mutual Respect

1st August, 1942.

Dear Bill (if I may be allowed)

On my departure from America, I am writing to tell you how extremely grateful I am for all the wonderful experiences that your organisa and kindness have made possible out here. I know that my visit has taken up a great deal of your valuable time; but I am also convinced that the valu I have obtained from the visit has been very great, and that we now know tha our minds and our Commands are working in the closest unity and along the same lines.

I am leaving tonight, and I leave with regret and very pleasan memories of everything I have seen here, and all the very nice people, both in your Command and outside, whom I have had the honour of meeting.

Anything I can do over the other side to help you and your affairs will be done, and you know that you have only to inform me and I sha be at your disposal on all occasions.

Finally, would you convey my best respects to Mrs. Lee and thank her for her kindness and hospitality and for the very kind present which she gave me for Mrs. Browning.

Yours ever

Boy Browning

Maj. Gen. F. A. M. Browning
Care British Joint Staff Mission
Offices of the Combined Chiefs of Staff
Washington, D. C.

My dear General:

I have just received your very nice letter of August 1 and I appreciated it more than I can tell you. I am confident that we understand each other thoroughly and that your visit will mean a very great deal in our own development. It certainly has been a valuable and pleasant experience for me.

I am going to Washington Friday to attend the conference in connection with the development of our new units and I shall expect rapid progress after that. I hope it will not be many months before I am with you again.

Mrs. Lee and Mrs. Chapman received the beautiful flowers that you sent, but not knowing your address, they wrote to you and sent the letters in care of Colonel Gaither of the Army Ground Forces. Colonel Gaither was away until after your departure and I am afraid that their letters were not delivered. If such is the case, please accept their thanks through me for your kindness and thoughtfulness.

I hope that I will see Tom Wells again before he goes, but if I shouldn't, I shall maintain close contact with you through him and I shall try to keep you informed of everything that we are doing. If my new command comes through, Colonel Chapman, my present Executive Officer, will be promoted to brigadier general and succeed me here. He is one of our finest and his ideas fit in with yours and mine perfectly.

It made me feel good for you to address me by my first name and when and if my promotion comes through, I hope to have the honor of calling you Boy. To you and to my friends in your command I send my sincerest regards and wish for you all nothing but good luck and success.

Cordially yours,

WILLIAM C. LEE,
Brigadier General, U. S. A.,
Commanding.

The British 1st Airborne Division was commanded by Frederick Arthur Montague (Boy) Browning, a handsome and proper British grenadier who had fought with distinction in World War I. He was married to British novelist Daphne du Maurier. Browning and Lee became fast friends almost from the beginning during Lee's first visit to England. Lee hosted him on an American visit and he is shown here inspecting the American airborne troops.

In a short 26 months, Bill Lee had brought the American airborne effort from a small test platoon of soldiers to two divisions.

18
Birth of the Airborne Division

1942

When General Lee returned from England, he set about developing specific recommendations concerning airborne divisions...

When my recommendations reached General McNair, he not only approved the organization of one division but of two, in order to provide an additional division for the Mediterranean area. He also approved the idea of a number of additional divisions to organize later. General McNair changed a number of details in the organization of divisions as recommended. He limited the number of men to approximately 8000 officers and men per division, and reversed the ratio of parachute and glider troops as recommended. I had recommended two parachute regiments and one glider regiment per division. General McNair changed this to two glider regiments and one parachute regiment. Although I talked to him later about this, I never did find out his exact reasons for this change. Apparently, he received some poor advice.

The 82nd Motorized Infantry Division, already up and running, was chosen to be the very first airborne division in the American Army. The choice of the 82nd merges mystery and myth. Omar Bradley was its commander, but he had been tapped to shape up a National Guard unit readying for combat at the same location. Consequently, the Division fell to Brigadier General Matthew Ridgway, whose star was already rising. General Ridgway was ambitious and had all the "tickets" to go to the top. He had worked for the Army Chief of Staff, General Marshall, several times, had already attended the Army War College, and had been promoted to his present position directly from the War Department. He knew his way around and made West Point exclusivity almost a cardinal rule.

The decision for the 82nd to become an airborne division must have hit him broadside, as there is no indication that he had ever given any thought to the unconventional airborne. Following quickly on that shocking news came another bombshell—a second airborne division would be created from the very loins of the 82nd. The other division, not yet activated, was to be the 101st Infantry.

General Lee had no idea that he would be chosen to take the 101st. In typical fashion, when the word came, he was both honored and humbled. On first blush, it appeared that the organizational arrangement was poised to become a can of worms. With any other single general in the Army, enormous ego problems would probably have ensued. Ridgway's volatility was no secret, and he had been known to relieve subordinates for a single perceived lapse in judgment. However, there is no evidence that Ridgway and Lee did not share the utmost respect for one another.

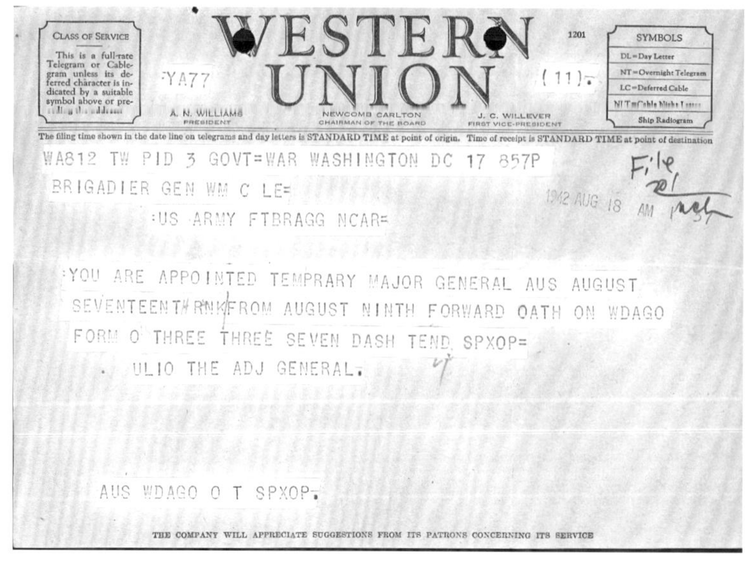

CLASS OF SERVICE
This is a full-rate Telegram or Cablegram unless its deferred character is indicated by a suitable symbol above or preceding the address.

WESTERN UNION

1201

SYMBOLS
DL=Day Letter
NT=Overnight Telegram
LC=Deferred Cable
NLT=Cable Night Letter
Ship Radiogram

YA77 (11)

A. N. WILLIAMS, PRESIDENT — NEWCOMB CARLTON, CHAIRMAN OF THE BOARD — J. C. WILLEVER, FIRST VICE-PRESIDENT

The filing time shown in the date line on telegrams and day letters is STANDARD TIME at point of origin. Time of receipt is STANDARD TIME at point of destination

WA812 TW PID 3 GOVT=WAR WASHINGTON DC 17 857P

BRIGADIER GEN WM C LE=

:US ARMY FTBRAGG NCAR=

1942 AUG 18 AM

File 201

:YOU ARE APPOINTED TEMPRARY MAJOR GENERAL AUS AUGUST SEVENTEENTH RNK FROM AUGUST NINTH FORWARD OATH ON WDAGO FORM O THREE THREE SEVEN DASH TEND. SPXOP=

ULIO THE ADJ GENERAL.

AUS WDAGO O T SPXOP.

THE COMPANY WILL APPRECIATE SUGGESTIONS FROM ITS PATRONS CONCERNING ITS SERVICE

Lee's knowledge of the airborne, his approach to leadership, and the high esteem in which his men held him turned aside all detractors. Bill Lee left the ego machinations to others.

The lineage for the 101st Airborne Division is traced to the 101st Division, formed on July 23, 1918, as part of the mobilization for World War I. At the end of the war, the unit was demobilized, but in 1921, the 101st Infantry Division was formed and reorganized as a reserve unit in Milwaukee, Wisconsin. On August 15, 1942, the division disbanded and was reactivated at Camp Claiborne, Louisiana as the 101st Airborne Division. General Lee reviews his troops.

Generals Ridgway and Lee

HEADQUARTERS 82D INFANTRY DIVISION
Office of the Division Commander

P/rp

Camp Claiborne, Louisiana
August 14, 1942

TO: The Officers and Enlisted Men of the 82d Infantry Division.

Tomorrow our destinies divide. That which was one Division, becomes two. That which was one team, must be rebuilt into two.

The relationship of our two divisions is unique. I know of no other case of a division dividing squarely in half, giving equally of all that it has of human ability and physical possessions. We have a common origin, and we anticipate a future of the closest association. Not only will we train side by side, but we hope and believe we will go to combat together, both resolved to contribute equally to a proud record of military achievement.

Records to date are the results of the earnest efforts of all - the results of team play, of team spirit.

It should be, and I am confident that it is the firm determination of every member of the Command to give his utmost in physical effort, in intelligence, and in character to the preservation and strengthening of that team spirit in the 82d, and to the creation of a like spirit in the 101st Division.

To every officer and man who tomorrow leaves the 82d for the 101st, I wish the best of fortune - may he be privileged to do for his new Division and its distinguished Commander, Major General William C. Lee, even more than he did for his old.

M. B. Ridgway

M. B. RIDGWAY,
Brigadier General, U. S. Army,
Commanding.

15 Aug

Personal Copy for
Major General Lee
M.B.R.

A Rendezvous with Destiny

The 101st Airborne Division, which was activated on August 16, 1942, at Camp Claiborne, Louisiana, has no history, but it has a rendezvous with destiny. Like the early American pioneers whose invincible courage was the foundation stone of this nation, we have broken with the past and its traditions to establish our claim to the future.

Due to the nature of our armament and the tactics in which we shall perfect ourselves, we shall be called upon to carry out operations of far-reaching military importance and we shall habitually go into action when the need is immediate and extreme. Let me call your attention to the fact that our badge is the great American eagle. This is a fitting emblem for a division that will crush its enemies by falling upon them like a thunderbolt from the skies. The history we shall make, the record of high achievement we hope to write in the annals of the American Army and the American people, depends wholly and completely on the men of this division. Each individual, each officer and each enlisted man must therefore regard himself as a necessary part of a complex and powerful instrument for the overcoming of the enemies of the nation. Each, in his own job, must realize that he is not only a means, but an indispensable means for obtaining the goal of victory. It is, therefore, not too much to say that the future itself, in whose moulding we expect to have a share, is in the hands of the soldiers of the 101st Airborne Division.

W.C. Lee
Major General, U.S.A., Commanding

19
101st Airborne Begins Intensive Training
1942

When the 101st Airborne Division returned to Fort Bragg in October of 1942, training the Division and getting them ready for combat was a mammoth task. General Lee, in coordination with the Parachute School, decided to begin training paratroopers by units. His feeling was that this would create a sense of pride and unit integrity. His insight proved exactly right as the "proof of the pudding" came in battle.

The beginning for a potential paratrooper started right in the frying pan—the reception station of the parachute school. This must have looked incredibly ominous to the young recruit. Driving into Fort Benning, home of the Infantry, the Queen of Battle, they traveled down a boulevard bordered with wonderfully manicured lawns and the massive buildings of the Army at its best—the officers' club, swimming pools, the landscaping, and in the distance, the stately infantry chapel with its red tiled roof. The contrast loomed in the distance in the form of gigantic steel towers, used exclusively for training paratroopers.

Training began with a grueling daily regime known as "parachute basic" and lasted thirteen weeks. Most of it was done in Alabama, across the Chattahoochee River, in complete isolation from the rest of the post. With uncanny foresight, General Lee had specifically secured the land for this purpose when he was commander of the Provisional Parachute Group.

Training was in four stages. Stage A was basic conditioning. The idea of this period was to weed out those who were not suited for the airborne. General Lee monitored this stage carefully; he understood the need for hard training, but also knew the necessity of keeping a leveling hand upon the sometimes overly exuberant instructors. During this time, the trooper would be up at four in the morning and have physical conditioning until noon. From one in the afternoon until six, it would be regular infantry training.

Stage B was regular paratrooper training—parachute packing, jump commands, parachute manipulation in suspended harnesses, parachute landing techniques, and the wind machine, which dragged the would-be paratrooper across the ground to teach him how to collapse a parachute in a ground wind. Add to all this the 34-foot tower that looked and felt like it was a thousand feet high. With the completion of this final trial, the hesitant young soldier suddenly began to feel that he was something special.

The next phase, stage C, involved the ominous towers seen by the young airborne volunteer as he entered the base. First came a couple of controlled descents, much like ones at the state fair. The third time the drop was for real—the free fall. The trooper was attached to a 38-foot canopy and manipulated it—pulling right on the risers, left, down, checking the wind, and preparing to land.

The last stage was rightly called D, as most of the youngsters were calling it D day. This was when the trainees exited the aircraft in flight. There were five qualifying jumps—the first four in the morning and the fifth jump at night. The trooper jumped in the morning and in the afternoon, the chute was repacked so he was ready for the next day.

Paratrooper training was probably the most difficult, grueling, challenging, and dangerous in the entire military. Is it any wonder that upon graduating, the young American paratroopers felt that they could leap any building with a single bound?

OPPOSITE TOP: Bill after a jump near Gallatin, Tennessee.

OPPOSITE BOTTOM: General Lee never stood on the sidelines. General James Gavin, probably the most famous World War II paratrooper and one of Lee's most ardent devotees, said it best: "...he was in touch with everything going on within his command. Men remember him as being everywhere, not just for ceremonies and inspections. He had a way of just 'popping up' and talking with NCOs and young officers ..."

This Is It!

TOP: The trooper's heart is pounding, his mouth is dry, his fear is palpable, and his adrenaline is pumping. Here is where all the training, the sacrifice, and the discipline reaches its apex. THIS IS IT!

BOTTOM: STAND UP; HOOK UP; SOUND OFF FOR EQUIPMENT CHECK.

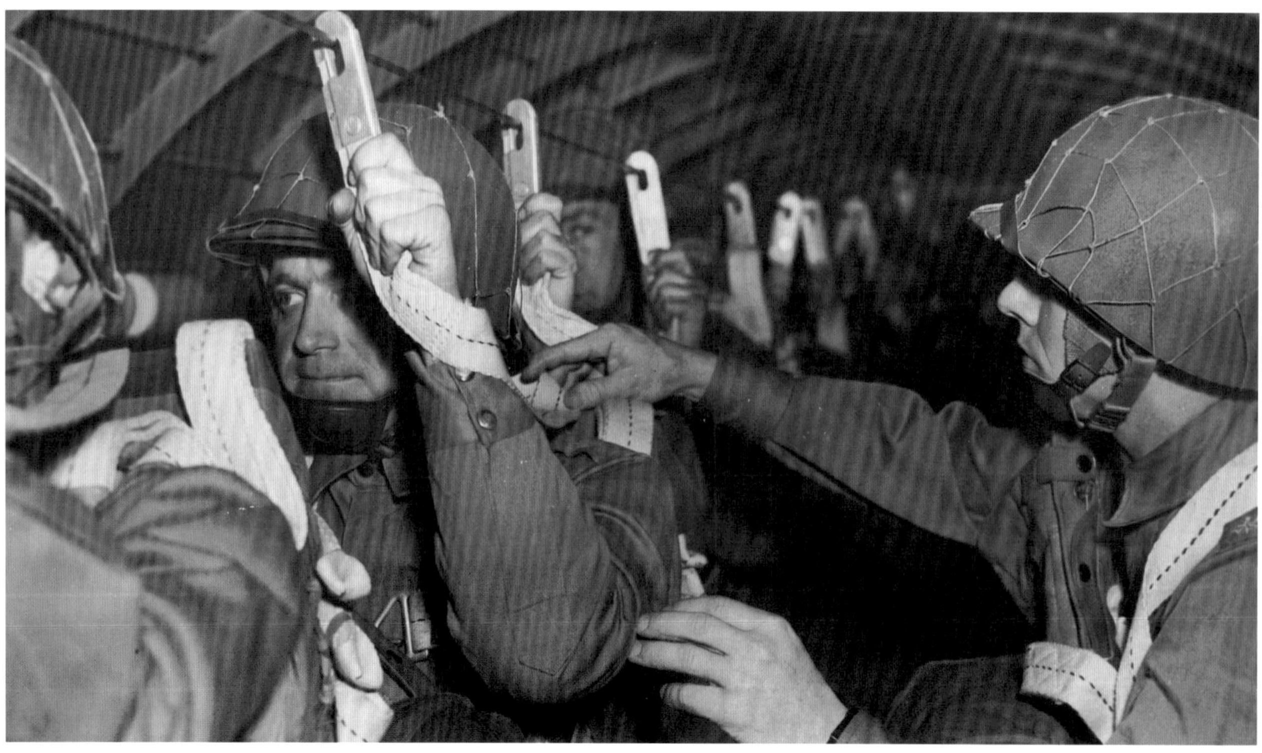

STAND TO DOOR. Now it's "Stand in the door." Remarkably, many of the early airborne training routines remain today.

GO!

OPPOSITE:
CHECK CANOPY.

PREPARE TO LAND

THANK YOU, LORD!

The generals review the troops. To General Lee's left is Eldridge Chapman, his replacement at the Airborne Command and his best friend. General Chapman, who later went on to command the 13th Airborne Division in Europe, jokingly commented in a letter that he often thought he was such a good friend because his first name was the same as Bill's father's. General Ridgway, Commander of the 82nd, is to his right. The 82nd is preparing to deploy to England.

20
101st Airborne Prepares for Combat

1943

When the 82nd Airborne Division was chosen to be the first to go into combat, the young airborne world was stunned. It had been assumed that Bill Lee, the premier airborne trooper, would receive the honor of leading the Airborne into combat. How and why the decision was made remains one of the mysteries of airborne development. Practically, it made absolutely no sense. Lee had been to Europe, had planned the role of the airborne, and had actually selected sites for training.

Conventional wisdom said that behind the scenes, General Ridgway, through his numerous contacts in the War Department, especially with General Marshall, simply outmaneuvered the gentle Southerner. Or that the Airborne was a small piece of the pie and staffers at the War Department did not think the plan through.

This inept chronicler's view is simply that Lee was thought to be indispensable in fathering the vast training and development of the Airborne yet to come. Although Bill Lee was now a Division Commander, his guiding hand could still remain with the parachute school and Airborne Command. Training paratroopers had to be continually refined, and integrating glider involvement was not even off the ground yet. Virtually everyone involved in airborne training were Lee men. Without a doubt, leaving Lee to train the troops proved to be sound wisdom as the 11th, 13th, and 17th Airborne Divisions were born.

If Lee resented the turn of events, he certainly did not show it and could not have been more gracious. He immediately pledged to do everything possible to help the 82nd prepare for the move to England. When they departed on April 20, 1943, Lee had fulfilled his commitment. He then turned his attention to training the troops knowing that his time would come.

HEADQUARTERS 82ND AIRBORNE DIVISION
OFFICE OF THE DIVISION COMMANDER

Fort Bragg, North Carolina
April 17, 1943

Dear Dava:

The Review and the delightful hospitality of your home leave most happy memories and the sending of flowers to Peggy was an exquiste act of thoughtfulness which touches me deeply.

One of the richest possessions I retain from the past six months of very full service is my respect, admiration and affection for you and Bill, sentiments which are fully shared by Peggy with me.

We look forward to renewed association in happier times.

Sincerely,

M. B. RIDGWAY,
Major General, U. S. Army.

LEFT:
Integrating glider training and delivering paratroopers by air was of great interest to General Lee. At every turn, he sought never to elevate parachutists above glidermen, who did not receive extra pay and often were not volunteers. General Lee took every opportunity to lobby for both. Having lost his battle on having airborne divisions with more firepower, he sought to use gliders more efficiently.

BOTTOM:
General Lee had the utmost respect for the Army Air Corps, and often remarked that without planes, paratroopers were reduced to walking. Troop Carrier Command, based near Indianapolis, had the task of training pilots who would fly the planes and gliders used by airborne troops.

Integrating Paratroopers, Equipment Delivery and Gliders

TOP: General Lee shares a laugh with General Hap Arnold, head of the Army Air Corps. At his left is possibly Colonel Fred Borum, commander of the Troop Carrier Command. This picture was taken at the Laurinburg/Maxton Army Air Base, one of four glider training sites.

BOTTOM: This operational demonstration was for the 79th Infantry Division.

Lee Was Proud of His Troops

RIGHT:

General Lee never missed an opportunity to show off his Division. Here a state legislator views a mass parachute jump at Bowman Field, Kentucky while the General explains the sequence of events.

BOTTOM:

One of General Lee's all-time favorite friends was Dr. J.W. Harrelson, Dean of Administration at North Carolina State in Raleigh. Dr. Harrelson had been Lee's mathematics teacher in 1917 and was the person that Bill sought for advice on whether he should stay in school or enlist to go to war.

ARMY & NAVY

PRODUCTION

Most Critical Occurrence

With pardonable pride, WPB announced that the U.S. had produced more than 7,000 military aircraft in May, would beat that total in June. With something less than pardonable reticence, it was mum about the rest of the military production program. It was not so bright a picture as WPB's announcement of aircraft production indicated it might be.

One day after the plane announcement, blunt Robert Porter Patterson, War Under Secretary, told the unpretty rest. In May, production of matériel for the Army Ground Forces had declined 3½% from the output of April. Actually, it had been scheduled to rise 2%. So it was a 5½% failure in production.

Said Bob Patterson: "This means that troops in training must be deprived of critical equipment. . . . If this situation continues even our overseas troops will suffer. . . . I . . . attribute the letdown . . . to overconfidence.

"Failure to appreciate the gravity of our situation . . . is evidenced by the coal strike, the Akron strikes and other stoppages . . . and by the tendency of certain manufacturers to divert too much time, thought and energy to the design and development of competitive civilian nonessentials. . . . The failure of May production is the most critical single occurrence in the Army Supply Program. . . . Failures to meet production in one month cannot be readily made up. . . ."

Only by aircraft's showing was the War Department pleased. Of the plus-7,000 planes delivered in May, around 5,000 were tactical types. The total number produced was up 40% from January, the weight (more bombers) up 63%. Barring failures, the U.S. was going to meet and pass its goal of 60,000 for this calendar year.

Bob Patterson's unspoken point was that wars are not fought by aircraft alone. Before Congress last week was the vastest military appropriation bill in history: a $71½-billion program for everything the Army will need in fiscal 1944, from dog food ($3½ million) to ammunition ($8 billion), guns, tanks, etc. ($6¼ billion) and aircraft ($23½ billion—the largest single item). With such a job ahead, neither labor nor industry could loaf for a minute.

U. S. Army Signal Corps

AIR-BORNE GENERAL LEE
Parachuting is safer.

TRAINING

Envelopment from the Sky

In the Tennessee maneuvers last week a full U.S. air-borne division was used in a tactical operation with larger units. Paratroops and glider-borne infantry carried out the attack. Riding with the gliderwen was TIME *Correspondent John H. Walker, who wrote this account.*

The air-borne attack was launched from Campbell Field, Ky., 100 miles northwest of the battlefield. In the grey mist big transports thundered down the runways closely spaced, each plane crammed with paratroops and each towing a bulky Army glider.

Now it was time for us to get moving. Major General William Carey Lee, division commander, who had invited me to ride with him, led the way to Glider 37, whispering mildly: "Well, here we go again." We piled in.

The tow plane started up before we were sitting down. A young lieutenant, settled on the benches running fore & aft on both sides of the glider, checking parachutes, barely got out in time. He lit running as the big 15-man glider, suddenly an amazingly skittish, lightfooted creature, lifted off the runway. To a glider novice the take-off was startling; we were air-borne and climbing on the rope while the heavier tow plane was still soaring down the runway, picking up speed for its own take-off. We climbed rapidly to 700 feet, circled to get into formation.

Candid Craft. The troop-carrying glider is a candid sort of aircraft, no secrets, nothing concealed. Canvas fabric covers the fuselage; in flight it vibrates like a drumhead. The whole craft is springy and alive as a new buggy. Pilot and co-pilot sit up in the blunt, transparent nose, a single row of instrument dials in front of them. The noise of rushing air is astonishing.

Controlling the flying boxcar on the end of the tow cable is not easy. Our pilot worked hard at it, carefully keeping us above the tow plane and out of its jolting prop-wash. He gripped the control wheel tightly, several times took one hand off to stretch his cramped fingers.

One thing had gone wrong right at the start; the undercarriage release gear

U. S. Army Signal Corps

GLIDER SQUADRON IN ACTION (bazookaman at right)
They ride to battle but walk back.

General Lee was very sensitive to the intense training requirements of glider troops and pilots. He was also keenly aware of the feeling of his paratroopers that somehow those who rode in gliders were inferior to those jumping out of planes. In his view, nothing could be further from the truth—men in gliders were helpless in controlling their destiny and they had only one chance to land. Lee often rode in gliders in exercises to demonstrate its safety and importance. Throughout all his experience, he never lost sight of the fact that parachuting and riding in the glider were only a secondary objective—carrying on the fight once on the ground was paramount.

Dearest Dava:

Attached hereto is a picture of the glider in which we crashed the other day. No one seriously hurt. Please keep this as a souvenir of 1943 maneuvers.

With much love,

Bill
Bill

Honey - I love you - sure did enjoy talking to you tonight - Call me soon
Bill

The Eagle Division

"The bald or American eagle is the national emblem of the United States of America. It is a symbol of our Republic and stands for all that speaks of vision, liberty, strength and victory.

The ancient armies of the Romans carried the symbol of an eagle as a standard for its victorious armies. In Greek mythology we find an eagle, attendant on Zeus, holding in its claws the lightning bolts of the gods. To this day the eagle is inevitably present in war and triumphant trophies.

... During battle [Old Abe, the eagle of Civil War fame] would fly up into the air to the length of his long tether, hover above the flags in the cloud of smoke, and scream encouragement to his human comrades.

The fame and glory of Old Abe and the Eagle Brigade live, not only in the traditions of the past, but in the design of our present Division insignia which colorfully portrays the famous War Eagle against a shield of black. Because our Division is Airborne, destined to fly into battle through the airlanes of the sky, the symbol of the great American Eagle seems to us especially appropriate."

OPPOSITE:
General Lee dedicates Young Abe. The eagle symbol was very important to paratroopers and to General Lee. In his famous "rendezvous with destiny" speech, he mentioned it: "Let me call your attention to the fact that our badge is the great American Bald Eagle. This is a fitting emblem for a Division that will crush its enemies by falling upon them like a thunderbolt from the skies." General Lee created the credo of the "Eagle" division which exists today. In Vietnam, 101st Airborne Division soldiers assaulting enemy territory by helicopter always said, "The Eagle Is Landing."

RIGHT:
Bill Lee I, mascot of the 101st Airborne Division.

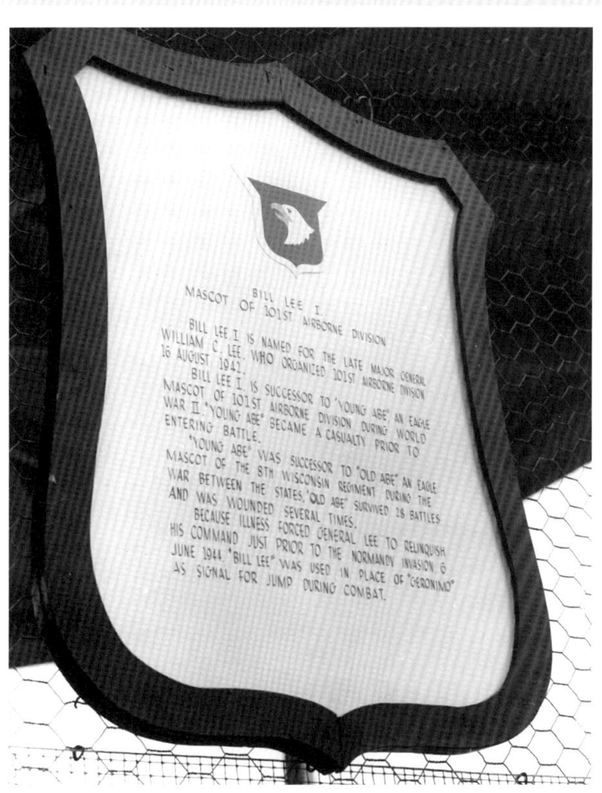

On to England

VI. Clothing, Equipment, Housing.

1. Baggage allowance is 77 lbs.

2. Heating is poor in England, rooms in the War Office are cold and damp as a result of destruction of glass of windows.

The following clothing is recommended:

Woolen OD uniforms,
Wool socks,
Medium weight long woolen underwear,
Pull over sweater,
Overshoes,
Long woolen OD overcoat,
Woolen muffler,
Rain coat.

3. Civilian clothes may be worn off duty in England. Blues are not necessary, OD is acceptable everywhere.

4. Take toilet articles with you. (Electric razor will not operate on British circuit.) Take abundant stock of cigarettes if you are a smoker; British brands are inferior and costly.

5. Hotels.

"Claridges", Crosvenor House, and the Dorchester are recommended.

VII.. Mail.

Officers' mail may be addressed to the War Department Foreign Mail Room, Room #1633, Munitions Building, Washington, D.C. Enclosed in this envelope should be a second envelope with a five cent stamp on it addressed to the officer's address at his overseas station.

The General is on his way to England ... "Very few people know it but in March, 1943, I was again ordered to London. I carried a small planning staff with me including my Div. G-3, his assistant, an aide, my air officer, and my assistant G-4. There I was briefed thoroughly on Overlord as it was to be presented to the President, the Chiefs of Staff, and Mr. Churchill a little later in Washington. I had long talks with COSSAC staff, General Morgan, General Browning, and Field Marshall, Sir Allan Brooks, C. of S., British Army. ... Again I recommended that American Airborne troops be upped. It was planned at that time to use only the 101st, but by the time the plan was presented to the Chiefs of Staff, the American Airborne Contingent had been upped by several additional parachute regiments. At that time, the 82nd had been ordered to Africa and it was assumed they would not be available for the cross-channel invasion."

Whenever an officer is promoted, the military insisted that a new photograph be taken and placed in his official military file. Bill sent this one to Dava with a note on the back: "To my dear wife with a heart full of love."

December 21, 1942

SEASONS GREETINGS
TO: Officers, Warrant Officers
and Enlisted Men,
101st Airborne Division.

In years past, the Christmas Season has turned our thoughts in reverence and joy to the birth of the Prince of Peace; to reunions with our loved ones at home; to feasts, and to merriment. This year we are engaged in a war for our very existence. Most of us will, of necessity, forsake the usual reunions with our loved ones; many of the joyful activities of other Christmas Seasons will be missing. But as we think of the sacrifices we are making along with those of our comrades in arms in the jungles of Guadalcanal, on the sands of the African desert, and in every corner of the globe, the Christmas Season this year should impart to us a deeper significance than ever before. Upon the success of our efforts depends the survival of those principles for which Christ worked and died; the security of our families and friends, and the spirit of freedom that forms a basis for the American way of life.

To every officer, warrant officer and enlisted man of this Division I extend my best wishes for the Holiday Season, and join with you in the sincere hope that through our success we shall establish a universal permanence to the words of Christ, "Peace on Earth, good will toward men."

W. C. Lee

U.S.
U.S.

Planning for Operation Overlord was constant. It was during this time that General Lee wrote the airborne doctrine for the invasion. He was working day and night, and an aide commented that he went for long periods without sleep. With General Lee are Brigadier General Don Pratt, his assistant division commander; chief of staff for General Bradley; and Field Marshall Bernard Montgomery.

21
Back to England
1943

As the 101st Airborne Division honed its skills and endured several false starts for getting into the war, General Lee was ordered to England for planning purposes again in May of 1943; the cross-channel invasion had been approved by the Allied Command. During the planning sessions, anxiety abounded—the invasion's success was more than probable but the possibility of failure was unthinkable. An eye witness observed, "Lee's confidence in his paratroopers and past knowledge of the fighting terrain was absolutely essential in calming the fears of the chief of staff, supreme allied commander (COSSAC)." Lee said, "When the area beaches of Normandy and the Cotentin Peninsula came into focus, armor was not feasible because of the soft sand but it was tailor made for paratroopers."

It wasn't the most opportune time for General Lee to be away from his Division. Prophetically, the 101st was engaged in the South Carolina and Tennessee maneuvers designed by the General to employ the very contingencies which were being discussed in the Normandy invasion planning sessions.

General Lee returned to the States only to be ordered back two months later to prepare for the Division's arrival and the invasion. "I took several members of my staff with me and we set up in London an airborne planning agency under General Devers, Theatre commander. Here we were again briefed on Overlord. In the meantime, I went to the Mediterranean areas to observe airborne operations in Italy. On my return to England, in September, only part of the Division had arrived. It all got there in late September or early October. During this period in England, before and after the arrival of the Division, I attended many conferences on Overlord and other tentative emergency and alternate preparations. The conferences were held at General Devers' headquarters and COSSAC, and later with Generals Bradley, Eisenhower, Leigh-Mallory, Browning, and Montgomery. These conferences were continuously being held, and I cannot remember the exact one in which the division was given its mission, but it was given to me personally by General Bradley in November or December, 1943, at the headquarters, although we had talked it over many times before."

The super-human schedule of General Lee involved coordinating military exercises, planning for the invasion, conferences, meetings, and dealing with divisional problems. The Screaming Eagles arrived at Liverpool on September 15, 1943 and moved to Wiltshire and Berkshire, and for the next 10 months, intensive unit training was the order of the day. The schedule was grueling.
Working six and seven days a week, they trained on Salisbury Plain, the same place that Captain Lee had been in 1932 and 1935.

General Lee drove his troops as relentlessly as he drove himself. Their training included hikes of 25 miles or more in full combat gear, which the General often led himself. His joke to the men who accepted the back-breaking schedule was always, "This is better than plowing a mule on my farm in Dunn."

General Lee directed the formation of the Division's own jump school, and by the time of the invasion, the school had trained over 400 officers and men. He established a pathfinder group of select courageous paratroopers to jump in advance of the main party and communicate with the pilots of the invasion force. Pathfinders saved hundreds of lives and proved to be a stroke of genius.

Operation Eagle

TOP:
Field Marshall Montgomery visits the 101st during night training.

BOTTOM:
General Lee in Morocco with Brigadier General William Donovan.

General Lee accelerated the training of the Eagle Division. "We immediately executed several problems in which we landed just back of a simulated beach, took up an all-around defense, and assisted waterborne forces to land. This culminated in practice Operation Eagle, in which we jumped the parachute elements by night and brought in glider elements by truck (assumed to be gliders) to constitute the entire Division in an area just north of Newburg. I believe that this was in January, 1944. By this time we knew pretty well what our problem was to be and we could practice it throughout...General Bradley began to read himself into Overlord, he began to talk to his corps commanders. Although I was not a corps commander, my division was classified as army troops, and being the highest ranking airborne commander in England at the time, I think that I attended all these conferences. In addition, General Bradley had me in several times alone to talk over possible specific missions for our airborne....the areas for the allied landings had been definitely determined by that time. Also, it had been definitely decided that the British airborne was to support the British landings and the American airborne our own landings...by this time it had been decided to include Utah beach in the American landings and to support this landing by airborne support of the 101st and the 82nd, the latter having arrived in Ireland from the Mediterranean....about the middle of January, General Bradley called General Ridgway and me into his office and gave us our missions. These were as follows: 101st: to drop in hours of darkness on D-Day, H minus five, to seize and hold the causeways leading from Utah beach to the mainland and assist the landing of the waterborne troops; to destroy certain coastal batteries, to seize St. Mère Église, to protect the south flank of landing area (Utah beach); later to push across the Cotentin Peninsula and join up with the 82nd Division, and be prepared for several other lines of action.

"82nd: to drop on western side of Cotentin peninsula, seize certain areas and prevent enemy reinforcements from moving up the western side of the peninsula from the south. I believe that the 82nd was to drop the second night...due I believe, to Matt Ridgway's urging, the area and time of his drop was changed to the east side of the peninsula. This, of course, necessitated a change in certain portions of our own mission. We still had the principle mission of securing the causeways and thereby assisting and assuring the success of the landing of the waterborne troops. The general area of the drop was moved to the south somewhat and we were given the additional mission of capturing Carentan. The 82nd was to drop farther to the North."

HEADQUARTERS 82D AIRBORNE DIVISION
APO 469, U. S. ARMY

In the Field,
24 Sept. 1943

Dear Bill,

Doc brought me your letter. It touches me deeply. I shall treasure it. No more prized possession can come to a soldier. I tried to convey my feelings toward you when I was leaving Bragg. I think you knew them then, and know them now. They do not change.

It hurt me to even delay your visit but as I have explained to Gerry, the radio from AFHQ announcing your coming was received on the night prior to planned departure of our first serial on what would have been an historic mission. We had been given 96 hours to prepare it, and 48 of those had to go to air movement from TUNIS to SICILY. To have you and Gerry and be unable to turn myself and staff over to you would have been distasteful to you and keenly disappointing to me. Yet I could not have interrupted the work of those last vital hours. I felt that you would understand as of course you did. As soon as that plan was cancelled I sent a note to LEMNITZER to please ask you and Gerry to come at once. Between then and your arrival, I was given a new mission, this time with eight hours notice. You saw the outcome.

No one can follow your fortunes and those of your Command with the depth of sincerity and hopes for high achievement that all of us do in the 82d.

May our unique past service together be quickly re-established. God bless you Bill and give them Hell as I know you will.

Faithfully,

Matt

MATT

by RP Eaton C of S. Matt is out on his usual hike & Gerry cannot wait for his return.

General Lee Struck by Heart Attack

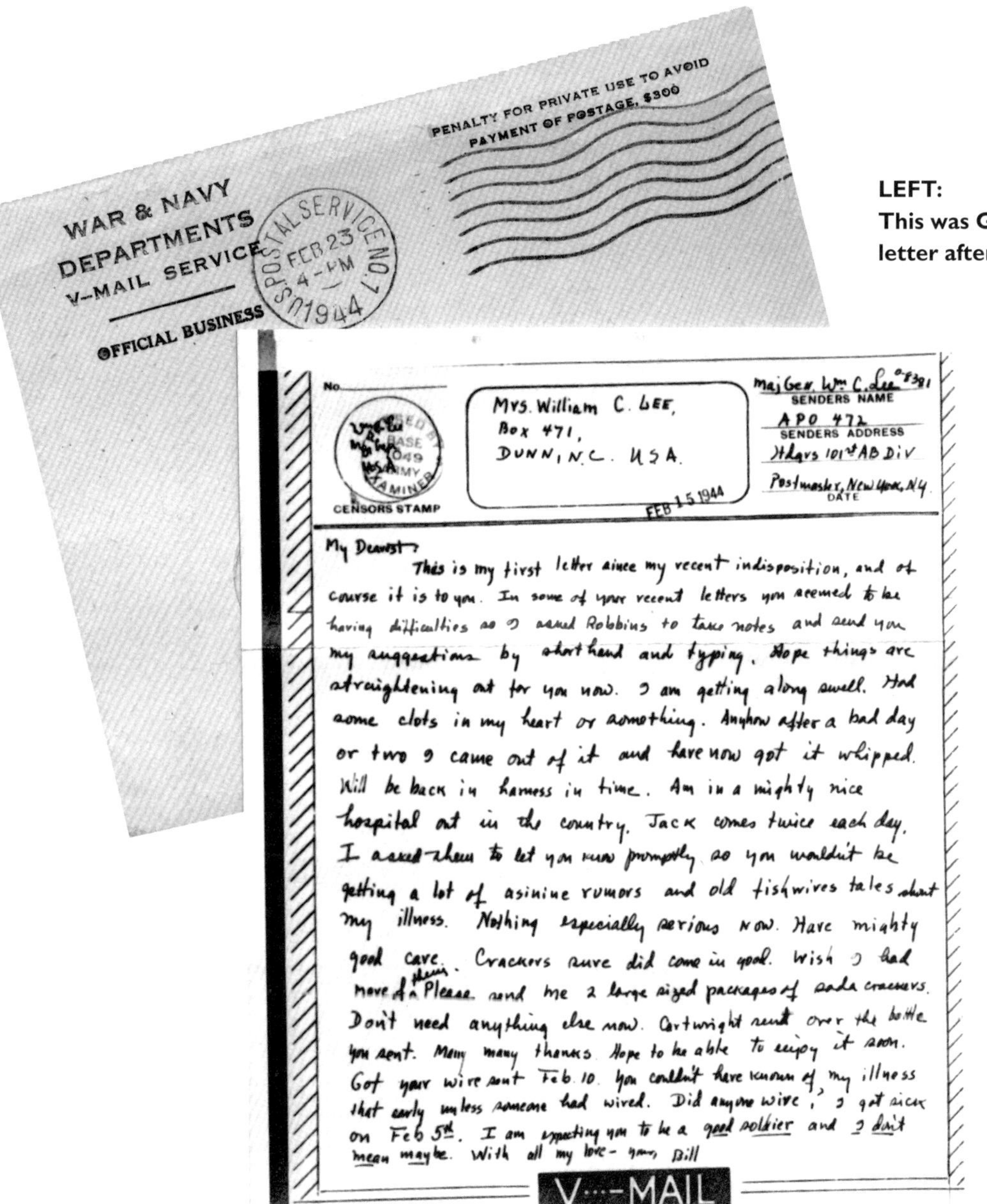

PENALTY FOR PRIVATE USE TO AVOID PAYMENT OF POSTAGE, $300

WAR & NAVY DEPARTMENTS
V-MAIL SERVICE
OFFICIAL BUSINESS

U.S. POSTAL SERVICE NO. 1
FEB 23 4-PM 1944

No.

Mrs. William C. Lee,
Box 471,
Dunn, N.C. USA.

Maj Gen Wm C. Lee O-8381
SENDERS NAME
APO 472
SENDERS ADDRESS
Hdqrs 101st AB Div
Postmaster, New York, NY
DATE

CENSORS STAMP

FEB 15 1944

My Dearest—
This is my first letter since my recent indisposition, and of course it is to you. In some of your recent letters you seemed to be having difficulties so I asked Robbins to take notes and send you my suggestions by shorthand and typing. Hope things are straightening out for you now. I am getting along swell. Had some clots in my heart or something. Anyhow after a bad day or two I came out of it and have now got it whipped. Will be back in harness in time. Am in a mighty nice hospital out in the country. Jack comes twice each day. I asked them to let you know promptly so you wouldn't be getting a lot of asinine rumors and old fishwives tales about my illness. Nothing especially serious now. Have mighty good care. Crackers sure did come in good. Wish I had more of them. Please send me 2 large sized packages of soda crackers. Don't need anything else now. Cartwright sent over the bottle you sent. Many many thanks. Hope to be able to enjoy it soon. Got your wire sent Feb. 10. You couldn't have known of my illness that early unless someone had wired. Did anyone wire? I got sick on Feb 5th. I am expecting you to be a good soldier and I don't mean maybe. With all my love— Your Bill

V-MAIL

LEFT:
This was General Lee's first letter after his heart attack.

February 15, 1944

My Dearest—

This is my first letter since my recent indisposition, and of course it is to you. … I am getting along swell. Had some clots in my heart or something. Anyhow after a bad day or two, I came out of it and have now got it whipped. Will be back in harness in time. Am in a mighty nice hospital out in the country. … Crackers sure did come in good. Wish I had more of them. Please send me 2 large sized packages of soda crackers. … I got sick on Feb. 5. I am expecting you to be a good soldier and I don't mean maybe. With all my love—

Your Bill

AIRBORNE

Maj Gen W. C. Lee 0-8381
HEADQUARTERS 101st AIRBORNE DIVISION

OFFICE OF THE COMMANDING GENERAL

A.P.O. 472- Postmaster, New York, N.Y. March 1 1944

March 1, 1944

Dearest:

Just a note today. Am still getting along fine. Am disgustingly healthy. Absolutely no news except that they shifted my bed around today so I could look out the window. I don't have much privacy these days and nights but am getting used to it now. I fret about having somebody around all the time because it isn't at all necessary, but I can't say too much because all they do is give me a sleeping pill and put the quietus on me pronto. Only have two more weeks in bed after this week.

Please see attached letter from Omar. Put it in our scrapbook and save it because someday he is going to be a mighty great man and we will be proud of his letter.

I think of you all the time. I know that you have kept a stiff upper lip through your trials and feel like I ought to be kicked good for being a source of anxiety to you. I shall try to make it up to you after this war is over and we can all come home.

I don't think much about when that will be because I want it to come so much.

Best to any who may ask,

With all my love—

Bill

12 March 1944

Dear General Lee:

Throughout the life of this Division as an Airborne unit, it has been closely and intimately associated with the 101st Airborne Division. In fact, I believe that the circumstances under which these two divisions came into existence, and which have attended so much of their training, are without parallel in our service. I am sure this is true of the understanding, the mutual respect, and the wholehearted cooperation which have unfailingly characterized their relations.

During this period of more than eighteen months, the members of the 82d Airborne Division have come to associate your name and leadership inseparably with that of the Division you have trained and led with such conspicuous success.

During those eighteen months, there has developed among the members of this Division a deep respect for you as a soldier, and an abiding affection for you as a man. They appreciate, as only soldiers can, the feelings you have doubtless experienced in having illness terminate your command of the 101st Airborne Division.

They wish you to know these things. They also wish you to know that in the recognition of duty superbly performed there is likewise recognition that to restore you to health is now the first consideration.

With the sincere hope that this will be quickly and fully accomplished, the members of the 82d Airborne Division salute you with warmth of heart.

Sincerely,

M. B. Ridgway

M. B. RIDGWAY,
Major General, U. S. Army.

Dear Matt,

I have just received your letter of March 12th, which incidentally was my 49th birthday.

Your letter has touched me very much indeed and I cannot find words to express my deep appreciation for your kindness and thoughtfulness. I assure you that my heart is very close to all the officers and men of the 82d Division and I shall exalt in your successes and in the very fine job that I know your division is going to do.

My heart is too full to try to say more, but I do want to take this opportunity to thank you for the spirit of cooperation and helpfulness which you have always shown in my dealings with you. It is my sincere hope and wish that the future will bring us together again.

Sincerely,

WILLIAM C. LEE,
Major General, USA.

Form 10.

WESTERN UNION 2 33

CABLEGRAM

(THE WESTERN UNION TELEGRAPH COMPANY)

(Incorporated in the State of New York, U.S.A., with limited liability).

RECEIVED AT 22 GREAT WINCHESTER STREET, LONDON, E.C.2.

M7107 DUNN NCAR 61 75 32=

EFM

WILLIAM C LEE 08381
AMICEL LONDON= 1610 .U.

YOU ARE MORE THAN EVER IN MY THOUGHTS AT THIS TIME HOPE YOU ARE IMPROVING ALL MY LOVE DEAREST.

:DAVA JOHNSON LEE.

Even after his illness, General Lee maintained a vigorous schedule. He traveled to Pope Field for a special ceremony at the urging of his friend, General William Old. Early on, General Old had supported General Lee's ideas of a strong marriage between his paratroopers and the Air Corps.

22
Illness & Retirement

1944-1947

On February 5, General Lee had a debilitating heart attack. At first, he discounted it as not being serious and fully expected to return to his command. This proved not to be the case. In March, it was confirmed that in order to save his life, Lee must return to the States for further recuperation. General Lee protested, but when he had another attack, he had to conclude that his physicians were right, and he would never allow his own ill health to jeopardize the mission and possibly hurt his beloved men. He felt there were many capable men who could lead his Division into battle. After a short stint at Walter Reed Hospital, General Lee returned to his home at 209 West Divine Street, Dunn, North Carolina and was officially retired in December of 1944.

This period of General Lee's life was understandably very distressing, as he was the consummate soldier. While in England and Walter Reed, and later in Dunn, he received thousands of letters. Even from his sick bed he often responded and constantly thought of those he had left behind. His physical heart was damaged, but in another sense, it was also emotionally broken. Missing the big show was, by his own admission, the greatest disappointment of his life.

A Sick General Bounds Out of Bed

By LOWELL M. LIMPUS

Dunn, N. C., June 11.—News that U. S. paratroopers changed their traditional war-cry from "Geronimo" to "Bill Lee," as they leaped from their planes over Normandy, brought a sick man right out of his bed here this afternoon. The father of American parachute work wasn't forgotten, even if he couldn't be with his boys when the big test came.

The sick man was Bill Lee, himself—more formally known as Gen. Lee. He was at home, on leave from Walter Reed Hospital, when some of his own fighting men swung the spot light on their absent leader. They did it when, speaking from the front by radio on the Army Hour, they told how they had switched their battle cry, as they went into action to honor their sick commander.

Suffered 2 Heart Attacks.

The medical officers insisted on sending Gen. Lee back, despite his vigorous protests, to recuperate after two successive heart attacks. He was in bed this afternoon, when some of his own men came on the air. His wife, Daza, happened to be listening and she ran to tell the invalid. The news brought him out of bed in a rush and she couldn't do a thing with him as he bent over the loud-speaker.

Gen. Lee frankly choked up, overseas describing how they sprang to the attack shouting his name.

Organized Paratroopers.

The action of the paratroopers was easily understood by his fellow officers, however. They know what his men think of Major Gen. William C. Lee, the middle-aged commander, who insisted on jumping with every class in the early days of the parachute school—and who kept right on jumping even after he had been badly hurt doing so.

And they know just how much his country owes to Bull Dog Lee.

He gave us our air-borne organization by sheer persistence in the days when nobody seemed to care about it. He built our first parachute school, organized the first parachute battalion, trained out first air borne command and then

Gen. Bill Lee
Remembered by his boys.

borne Division—one of the outfits that the Germans have identified

A Visit to Fort Benning

Although not fully recovered, General Lee still maintained involvement with the Airborne. Here he inspects paratroopers at Fort Benning in March of 1945 as the war is winding down.

ABOVE:
The Doffermyres accompanied the Lees to Fort Benning. Doctor Doffermyre was Bill's very good friend and was concerned about his health, which may have been the reason he came along on this trip.

Major General W. C. Lee,
Dunn, N. C.

My Dear General Lee:

I am sending you this article which appeared in the Bayonet on March 15. I am sending a duplicate copy of this letter and another copy of the clipping to your other address, hoping that one of these two will reach you without delay.

By this time you should have received three sets of the photographs that were taken during your visit here at the School. Some of these are not as good as they should be, others are extremely good likenesses of you: In any case, I am sending them all to you so that you can keep them as a memento of your visit. The extra sets are sent in the thought that possibly you might want to give some to the Doffermyers and have a duplicate set for yourself.

Your visit here was an inspiration to all of us. We are hoping soon to hear the good news that you will be on active duty again in the near future.

All of your good friends here join me in sending their best regards to you and Mrs. Lee.

Yours sincerely,

George V. H. Moseley Jr.

GEORGE V. H. MOSELEY, JR.,
Colonel, Infantry,
Acting Commandant.

Lee Stays Active

ABOVE: General Lee continued to get updates on the military. He often said that when he retired, he expected to wear only his work overalls.

BELOW: Lee often played host to distinguished visitors at his home. This occasion was to commemorate the fourth anniversary of the first airborne landing in Sicily. Shown are generals James Gavin, at the time commander of the 82nd Airborne; Maxwell Taylor, General Lee's successor in the 101st; and Jerry Higgins, one of General Lee's righthand men through the years. All three men frequently acknowledged their great debt to Lee.

Citation

North Carolina State College of Agriculture and Engineering

of the

University of North Carolina

CHANCELLOR JOHN WILLIAM HARRELSON:

Mr. President, I have the honor to present WILLIAM CAREY LEE, Major General, United States Army, of Dunn, North Carolina.

General Lee was born in Dunn, North Carolina, prepared for college in the public schools of Dunn, attended Wake Forest College, and was graduated from the North Carolina State College of Agriculture and Engineering. He attended the first officers training camp in 1917; was commissioned a second lieutenant in the Infantry Reserve on August 15, 1917; and served with the American Expeditionary Forces in Europe until the close of World War I. He was appointed a captain in the United States Army on July 1, 1920, and was promoted to the successive ranks, attaining that of Major General on August 18, 1942. He is a graduate of the Infantry School, the Tank School and the Command and General Staff School. The magazine TIME states that Major General William Carey Lee, father of United States Airborne doctrine, trained the One Hundred and First Division to a razor edge for the Normandy invasion, and because of illness, was compelled to give up the command.

General Lee's citation for the distinguished service medal includes the following: "For exceptionally meritorious and distinguished service rendered in a duty of great responsibility while organizing and establishing the Airborne Command . . . . . With meager facilities, a few partially trained instructors, and by exceptional ability, force of character, and the will to get the job done, he built the framework for a powerful striking force. . . . "

I commend him to you as well worthy of the honorary degree of Doctor of Military Science.

PRESIDENT FRANK PORTER GRAHAM:

WILLIAM CAREY LEE, upon the recommendation of the faculty of this College, and by vote of the Board of Trustees of the University of North Carolina, we confer upon you the degree of Doctor of Military Science, with all its rights and privileges.

Chancellor J.W. Harrelson presents the honorary degree to General Lee, who had been too ill to attend the ceremonies. To General Lee's left is Graves Vann, a good friend and fellow student at Wake Forest. Both transferred to North Carolina State after their sophomore year and roomed together.

Lee Returns to Fort Bragg

Although General Lee's health had begun to deteriorate and many cautioned that he was still attempting too much, he traveled to Fort Bragg to be honored by the 82nd Airborne Division. General James Gavin, the personification of the World War II airborne warrior and a true hero, felt that he owed it all to General Lee. General Lee had cut through bureaucratic red tape to bring Gavin into the Airborne and had nurtured him in his Provisional Parachute Group. General Gavin said often that it was General Lee who allowed him to grow while saving and protecting him from himself. A long list of airborne pioneers echoed this feeling.

July 8, 1944

Dear General Lee:

They were excellent soldiers and a superior fighting outfit, but we met them and made them yell uncle. They heard the name "Bill Lee" shouted in a more terrifying manner than they ever heard "Heil Hitler."

Best regards from the men and officers of the 1st Bn.

Lt. Col. P.F. Cassidy, 502nd Parachute Infantry

23 Correspondence

1944-1945

In Bill Lee's time, people wrote letters much more often than they do today, but even at that time, the quantity of Bill's correspondence must have seemed abundant. The letters in this chapter, many of which were written soon after his heart attack on February 5, 1944, are a few of many that he sent and received, and they show the respect and caring people felt for him and he returned to them.

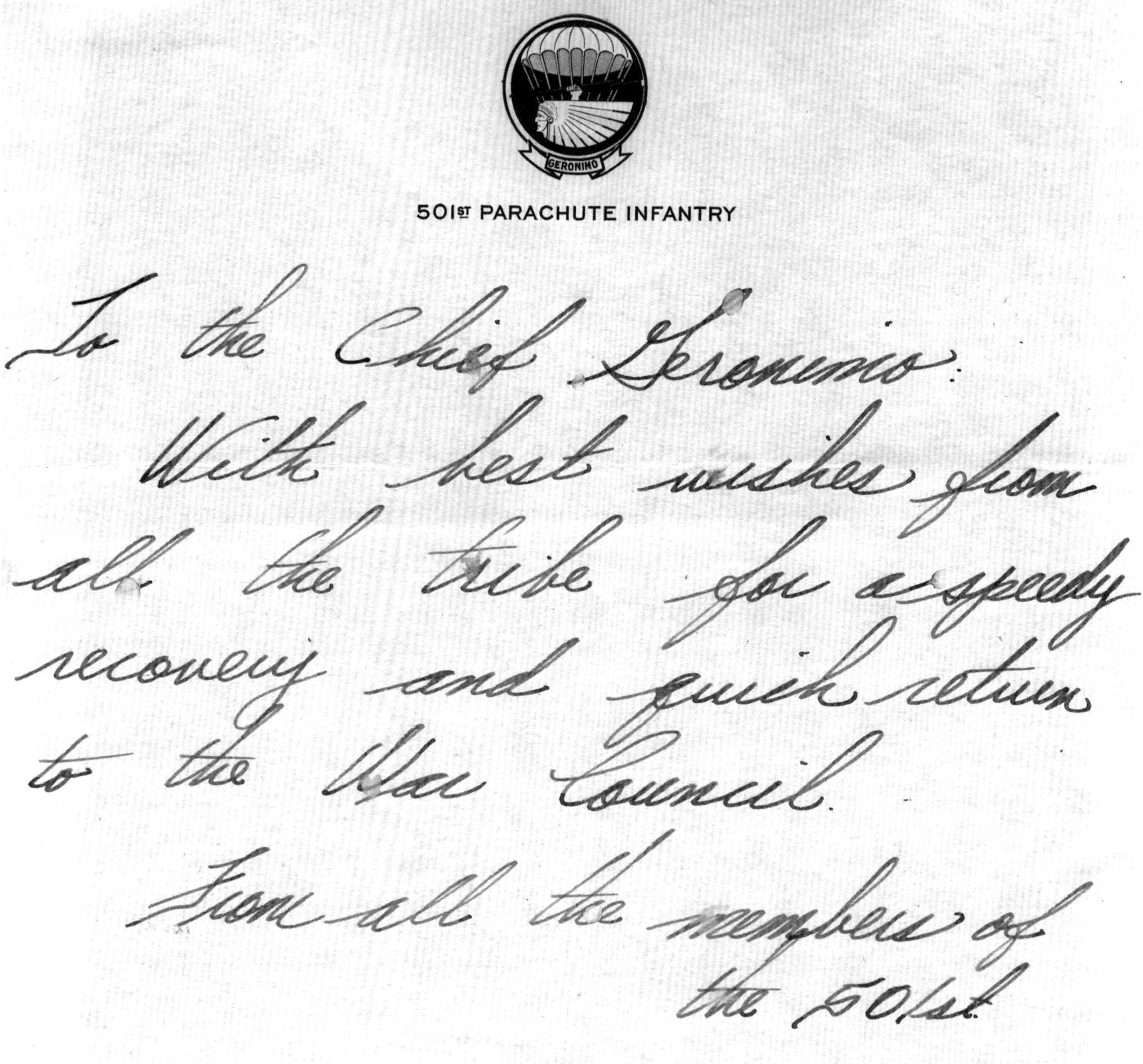

GERONIMO

501ST PARACHUTE INFANTRY

To the Chief Geronimo:
With best wishes from all the tribe for a speedy recovery and quick return to the War Council.
From all the members of the 501st.

February 5, 1944
Dunn, N.C.

Dear Bill,

I have been hopeing that you and I would get a chance to go hunting this season. There are plenty of birds and scarcely any hunters. The quail and wood cocks are huddled together, and there is two and three rabbits in one bed. There is scarcely any shells to shoot with so when I shoot them I try to double up on them and get two at one time. By myself I am more of a pot shot than a sport.

Bill, I am working hard doing some real farming. I'm growing a lot of grain and food.

I long to see the day when you can come home and we can load up our old fishing tackles and drive down to Hollands Lake and drift out and stake down at the "Old smoke house" and throw out and hear the stopper pop, that will be sweet music to me.

I think of you every day and I'm praying that you will have good luck. My wife mentions your name every time we make fresh pudding and sausage, I wish that you could drive by like you used to and get a sample of it, and I fell sure you will.

Yours truly,

Tom Godwin

W.J. Godwin

17 January 1944

Colonel Howard Johnson
501st Parachute Infantry

Dear Colonel Johnson:

General Lee has asked me to write and thank you, and through you, the officers and men of the 501st Parachute Infantry for the lovely flowers which he has received from you. It was certainly very thoughtful and very much appreciated.

I have just returned from the hospital and your "Chief Geronimo" is getting along fine.

Thanks to you and your tribe again for your thoughtfulness.

Jack E. Robbins
1st Lieutenant, AGD
Aide-de-camp

17 February 1944

Mrs. Blanche Grantham
Dunn, North Carolina

Dear Blanche,

I am indeed grieved to learn of Mr. Grantham's death and I extend to you and Emily and George my deepest sympathy. In addition to being a life long neighbor and friend of the family, Mr. George was one of my closest personal friends and I shall miss him a very great deal indeed in the days to come. There is no need to tell you what a grand old man he was and what a great influence for good he was in our community and in the building of our town. He was a very great soul and one that will be remembered in the annals of Dunn and Harnett County for years and years to come.

William C. Lee

18 February 1944

Lieutenant General F.A.M. Browning
Brigmerston House, Milston

Dear Boy,

Since seeing you last it has been my misfortune to have suffered what might be called a heart attack. I am now in an American Station Hospital at Hermitage, near Newbury. I am getting along splendidly and hope to be out of here within two or three weeks. I don't think anything serious is wrong with me and I am absolutely confident that I will be back in harness doing full duty in very short order so please don't let them sell me short for the invasion.

If, when passing, you can find time to drop by I will be deeply grateful.

William C. Lee

23 February 1944

Dear General Lee:

Dava called me when she first heard of your illness. I told her to buck up, that you had to get well and be your old self again and I was sure you would. Now Dava says that you are well on the way to recovery. You have some constitution!

Dava now is afraid you won't lie still and do what you are told. I hope you are ordered to stay quiet. You aren't that hard to manage, are you?

It is beautiful and springlike today. I have been out raking and trying to burn up the trash but the grass was too wet to burn. My crocuses and daffodils are way up.

England in spring must be lovely--things just grow in that climate, like they do here on the west coast.

... Dava seemed in much better spirits in her last letter. She is very brave.

I was so shocked to hear about you as Van had just written to me about how well you looked and how chipper you were.

Please take it very easy for Dava and everyone's sake and you will be your old self again. ...

Kay Moseley

A.P.O. 469, U. S. Army
18 February 1944

Dear Bill:

Your illness distresses me greatly, though I hear that you are much improved. I have delayed writing you in the hope that I could find time for a personal visit, but the days fly by, and I still see little chance of coming down in the near future.

Please know you are much in our thoughts and that you have our warmest and sincerest hopes for a prompt and full recovery. I shall come down at my first opportunity. Meanwhile, if there is anything I can do, officially or personally, you know it will give me much pleasure.

Faithfully,

M. B. RIDGWAY,
Major General, U. S. Army.

Major General W. C. LEE,
A.P.O. 472, U. S. Army.

HEADQUARTERS 101st AIRBORNE DIVISION

OFFICE OF THE COMMANDING GENERAL

March 24, 1944

Dear Bill:

Thought you might be interested in hearing about yesterday's show which went off very well indeed. We had the Division massed as guard of honor on the slope of the hill west of the Welford jump field. I brought the party out from the station to the field--six cars in all carrying Ike, Bradley and several lesser lights who accompanied the PM. The old man was in fine form--looked just like the cartoons, hat, cigar and all. He sabotaged our tight time schedule by insisting on walking around the troops instead of riding--went right down the first rank with the officers faced about to watch him.

After trooping the line he went back to receiving stand, climbed in a command car and had the men close in for a brief speech. He didn't say anything particularly memorable but the men got a big lift from seeing and hearing him.

Tony had arranged a glider and equipment display a few yards from the review field where they landed--4 loaded gliders. The personnel got out in good style and went into a simple tactical situation. Along the edge of the field was a display of airborne weapons and equipment which we used as a filler while we waited for the parachute formation.

The ships came in just about on schedule and the jump was really a beautiful one to watch. The day was perfect and the men floated down in the ploughed fields of the DZ. The PM had never seen such a large jump and enjoyed it immensely. We mounted up in command cars and rode through the DZ, watching the new men assemble. They were all extremely alert and gave a fine impression of superb physical condition.

We may have over-reached ourselves because on the way back to town the PM asked if he could come back next week and bring Mrs. Churchill. We'll have to arrange for a Parliamentary crisis.

Well Bill, you've been the source of a lot of worry to your many friends both here and in London but we're mighty glad to know you're on the upturn. Both General Eisenhower and General Bradley send their very best regards and hope to visit you when you're able to see them. General Bradley brought you a picture which I'm sending over.

Take good care of yourself and we'll all be around when you're ready to have us.

Sincerely

Max Taylor

From Lieut.-Gen. F.A.M. Browning, C.B., D.S.O.

Headquarters Airborne Troops (Main),
Home Forces.
28th February, 1944.

Dear Bill

Thank you very much for your letter of 18th February.

I am delighted to hear that you are getting g. I should have been down to see you before , but I was warned off.

I have to go to Scotland towards the end of week, and directly I get back from there I will and see you. In the meantime, take it easy; get impatient, there is plenty of time.

Yours ever
Boy.

CABLE ADDRESS: "WALDORF, NEW YORK" / ELDORADO 5-3000

The WALDORF-ASTORIA
PARK AND LEXINGTON AVENUES / 49TH AND 50TH STREETS / NEW YORK

Thursday Night

Dear General:

By the time you get this, I will probably be on the way. As far as I know, this is my last night here--and I am enjoying it.

Everything is going ok, but have been working night and day. I have been assigned as Squadron Commander for more than 250 EM, and that's some job.

Have been giving security lectures, checking service records, etc, but I like working with troops. Only have two 2nd Lts. to assist me. My job is to deliver the EM on the other side.

This is the first night I have been out and will be the last.

Hope you are feeling well again and that everything is going ok. Please give Mrs. Lee my regards. Am writing my folks a letter telling them I'm going.

See you after the war. Good luck. Sincerely,

PSN Just been upstairs talking with Former President Herbert Hoover. He's a fine old fellow.

ABOVE:
This letter was from Lt. Hoover Adams, Dunn, North Carolina.

Dear Bill,

I want you to know how sorry I am that I could not attend the decoration ceremony today. I am sure that you will appreciate how much I wanted to be there and how urgent the affairs were that kept me away.

Please accept my heartiest congratulations on the award to you of the Distinguished Service Medal. I consider it as especially well merited not only for the services that you have rendered as described in the citation, but also for the outstanding job you have done since you have been under my command.

Sincerely,

Bradley
O. N. BRADLEY,
Lieutenant General, U.S.A.,
Commanding.

Major General William C. Lee,
Headquarters 101st Airborne Division
APO #101, U. S. Army.

Farewells

24 February 1944

Staff Sergeant Herman J. Smith,
101st Airborne Division

Dear Sergeant Smith

I want to take this opportunity to thank you and your cooks, Sergeant Dale T. young and Corporal Foy T. Hodges, for the very fine soup and other things which you have been sending to me by Lieutenant Robbins during my present illness.

Everyone here who has tasted the soup and other dishes which you have sent have marveled at the perfection of its preparation and cooking, and have praised it very highly. Needless to say, it has been a godsend to me.

Will you please accept my very grateful thanks and express to Sergeant Young and Corporal Hodges my very deep appreciation for their thoughtfulness and kindness. I hope to thank them in person in the very near future.

William C. Lee

16 March 1944

Colonel Robert F. Sink,
506th Parachute Infantry

Dear Bob,

The doctors have informed me that the heart attack which I suffered recently has incapacitated me for further active service ... I am sure as a soldier that you will understand how disturbing this news was to me, but since there is no help for it, there is nothing to do but accept these new conditions and make the best of it.

... I am taking this method of expressing to you personally and through you to the officers and men of your command, my heartfelt and grateful appreciation for the loyal and superior work which you and they have performed while under my command.

I can remember the day that you were informed that you were to take over the command of the 506th Parachute Infantry. I told you at the time that I considered you one of the best soldiers that it had ever been my good fortune to know. Since that time nothing has ever happened to cause me to change my opinion in any way whatsoever. You have a magnificent regiment, most ably commanded and officered and I have every confidence that it is going to do a magnificent job against the enemy.

May God bless every one of you and bring you all through the days ahead safe and victorious. With deep personal affection, I am,

William C. Lee

16 March 1944

Colonel George V.H. Moseley, Jr.
502nd Parachute Infantry

Dear George,

... I am taking this method of expressing to you personally and through you, to the officers and men of your command, my deep and grateful appreciation for the loyal and superior work which you and they have performed while under my command.

Because of my peculiarly close and intimate association with your regiment, even before the Airborne Command and airborne divisions came into being, I have always had an especially soft spot in my heart for the 502nd. My confidence in the regiment and in you personally has never wavered. ...

William C. Lee

2 April 1944

Brigadier General Anthony C. McAuliffe
101st Airborne Division Artillery

My dear Tony:

As the time for my departure from this theater nears, I am taking this method of expressing to you my grateful and lasting appreciation for the magnificent work which you have done in the 101st Airborne Division. Without your aid, I am absolutely certain that the fine state of training, discipline, and morale which exists in this division, could not have reached the high standard which characterizes all of our units. The division is not Bill Lee's division or Don Pratt's division, but is Bill Lee's division and Don Pratt's division and Tony McAuliffe's division all inclusive. I am completely proud of the 101st Airborne Division and I have the utmost confidence that in the difficult days ahead, it is going to acquit itself with honor and cover itself with glory. Not to be able to be with you is the most bitter disappointment I have ever endured.

I want to commend you personally for the magnificent way in which you have trained and administered the Artillery units of this division. Your efficiency, character, loyalty and your splendid qualities of leadership have been and are such as to warrant your immediate promotion to the grade of Major General. Several times in the past I have made such recommendations and am again making the same recommendation, emphasizing those qualities which entitle you to this advancement.

... There is not much that one can say at a time like this except good-bye, good luck, God bless you and may He bring you safely home to your loved ones in due time. If there is anything that I can ever do for you, you know that you have only to call on me.

William C. Lee

6 April, 1944

Dear General Lee,

I want to tell you what a privilege it has been to serve as a battalion commander in your division.

You trained a great Airborne division and planned its use in combat. Our part shall be to carry out your plans, and we shall do it in a manner that will make you proud.

Your influence in this division extended much farther than to the officers. On many occasions you talked with the troops, individually and collectively. Each time you left inspired men.

I regret that there is not an opportunity to personally tell you good-bye.

G.L. Turner

9 April 1944

Major General William C. Lee

Dear Sir:

Among the greatest of your treasures should be the fact that is common knowledge among "your boys" that you overworked yourself in devotion to duty.

With an active mind, which has already made so many professional contributions to the war effort, I know you will feel challenged to carry on in such capacity as the fates decree and turn your thinking into channels of better futures for better Americans.

"Your boys" will all be expecting to see these contributions expressed at home after they have kicked that after-the-whistle-goal and cinched the game.

R.L. Bogard
Captain, 101 AB Div. Hq.

11 June 1944

Cleveland Heights, Ohio

Dear General Lee:

In listening to a description of the landing and invasion on the Army Hour this afternoon Mrs. Blazy and I pricked up our ears when the narrator stated that the troops, when they landed and charged the enemy, instead of the usual shout of "Geronimo" used "Bill Lee" as their battle cry, in honor of the pioneer in training paratroopers who is now in Walter Reed Hospital because of physical disability.

We regret to hear that you are ill and hope that it is nothing serious and that you may have a speedy recovery.

We also congratulate you on the substitution of your name for that of the Apache warrior, but, as we remember you, we do not recall anything that you have in common, in fact, quite the reverse.

Frank W. Blazy

All the Training Was Worth It

16 July 44

Dear Bill:

Here we are, doing business at the same old stand. I find today, being a Sunday, is the first time in weeks--literally--that I have a little time. So, hoping you will forgive me for not writing before, will attempt to bring you up to date on what has taken place.

First, you have every right to be tremendously proud of your 101st Airborne Division. They performed magnificently, from the lowliest private right on up. I knew we were going to do a good job, but I had hardly hoped for the outstanding one they did. Every commander from General Marshall on down has either written us a letter or verbally told us what he thought of our action. And you can bet we are one proud and cocky lot right now.

I think you probably know that the Division Headquarters Company, plus attached personal, received a unit citation. Bob S, Van, Skeets, and Ben W's all received them. Other units are in for it, and may or may not receive it.

Max received the British DSO, and the American DSC. Tony got the Silver Star, as did Bud H, Mike, Bob S, and Skeets. Bud M. received the DSC for the outstanding work he did, as a <u>platoon</u> leader rather than a G-3, due to the place he was dropped! Incidentally, his first parachute drop was the combat drop! Cool as a cucumber, and he did a whale of a job. Gathered about thirty-five men together, and fought his way back to the Division C.P., blowing up a German ammunition train, a German staff car, at least two 88's, and accounting for some thirty or forty Germans! Not bad for a tyro parachutist.

Bob C, of Van's organization, is in for the Medal of Honor as a result of a particularly fine job he did, <u>personally</u> leading a bayonet charge on a tough german position. You can imagine him doing just that, of course. And he succeeded, accounting for quite a few of the enemy. Not sure it will go through, but if not he will certainly get the DSC.

Pat C. got the DSC, and so did Doug Davidson, along with some twenty-eight others in the Division. All well deserved, too.

To answer your question about certain individuals: Don, Pappas, Grant, Turner, Vaughan, Carroll (from Skeet's unit) Rogers, Van Antwerp, Stubblefield, Eberle, Neilson, McReynolds, and--unconfirmed--Bob W from Bob S's outfit.

Time magazine. The papers have given a pretty good account of what happened there--it was a tough nut to crack, and a good deal of blood was spilled. We were up against the 17th Panzer Grenadier Division--SS Troops--and they were plenty tough. I had thought the "German Hitler Fanatic" was some newspaper propaganda, but it was not. They have a motto "Do or Die", and they died. I hate to tell you how many German bodies we had to haul out of that place after it was over, but we were over three days burying the dead. They wouldn't surrender. At first two or three would stand up and wave a white flag, and when the parachutists started forward concealed guns would open up from the flanks. Didn't take us long to learn that trick.

We both know we had no doubts about our parachute troops, and how they would fight, but, Bill, it would do your heart good if you could have seen how our Glider troops fought! They didn't intend to be left behind, and really covered themselves with glory! They took their casualties, and they dished out the punishment. There is no feeling between them now--both respect the other, and the parachutists are darn glad to call them buddies. In fact, they are now wearing the parachute boot--and there is no objection whatsoever from the parachutists!

As you can see from the above, we accomplished all jobs initially assigned; carried out subsequent assignments one day quicker than hoped for, and then took Carentan and the high ground both to the east and west thereof; held a tremendous sector and kept the 17th Panzer Grenadier Division, plus a German Parachute Regiment (the 6th) plus odds and ends of other units at bay for quite some time. It cost, but measured in terms of accomplishment, was worth it to the Allied cause many times over. As you can see from the fighting now, if the enemy had held Carentan we would have been in a critical state, as we could not have linked up the two beachheads.

Tony has done a grand job throughout--as a matter of fact, he commanded the Task Force that took Carentan from one side. Mozeley performed creditably when he took over, and as you know Mike M. led the outfit after Van was injured in the jump. Cox did a fine job, and turned out to be an excellent combat leader. Honestly, with one exception, all leaders turned in excellent if not superior jobs. You know about George W, I believe. Bud H took over his unit, and as I said, the gliders then made a name for themselves.

Well, I have rambled on for quite some time. I am writing up a history of our operation, with maps, and hope to be able to send you a copy of it if I can. Also, if I can get some pictures together, and they will permit me to send them, will include same.

My best to Dava, Helen, Henry and all my other friends in Dunn and vicinity. Tell General Chapman that Lt. Col. Hartel did a fine job while he was here, and his assistance was most appreciated. Here's hoping that you are taking life easy, that the fish are biting, and that good health is being enjoyed by one and all.

Sincerely, Jerry

In late December 1943, General Lee called in one of his outstanding young officers, Captain Frank Lillyman and gave him the mission of becoming yet another pioneer in the great airborne saga, that of developing pathfinders, whose mission was to jump first and direct the main bodies of paratroopers to their drop zones. Captain Lillyman wrote General Lee of his success:

25 July 1944
Major General Wm. C. Lee, U.S.A.
Dunn, N.C.

My Dear General Lee--

Can you remember when you've jumped in the number one position and as soon as the chute opened you looked back at the rest of them coming out the door and often heard the shout and yell in the air before the "chutes" developed? Its odd how you can hear the men yelling even with airplane engines buzzing.

Sometime between 0013 and 0015 on June 5-6, I went out the door over a jumpfield that didn't have a "safety crew" standing by on the deck. It was my forty-eighth jump and a rather important one, not only to me and my men but to the entire division.

As the silk filled and I turned to check the stick, not once, but eighteen times- the cry of "Bill Lee" filled the air over France. This, General, thirty seven minutes before there was another allied soldier on the Normandy peninsula.

The rest is history.

When I last saw you on the train I promised you that I, personally, would do my utmost to fulfill the confidence that you, as my division commander had placed in me to lead the Pathfinders in their all-important mission. I don't think I let you down General...

The whole group join me in sending their regards.

Respectfully,
Frank L. Lillyman

August 5, 1944

My dear General Lee:

Your good letter dated July 26th arrived yesterday. When Mike comes down to see me today, I shall lend it to him so that he and Bob and Steve and Pat may have a chance to read it. And no doubt Mike will want to have copies of the letter made so that the non-commissioned officers and privates, who did such a good job all the way through, will have a chance to read what you think of them.

I suppose you know that, two days before "D" Day, General Taylor addressed each regiment. Among other things, he directed that "Geronimo" was not to be the jumping word; that "Bill Lee" would be shouted. The officers and men unanimously and vociferously acclaimed this. And I want you to know that as I stood in the door of the lead ship of the leading battalion lift, with the red light on, and the inundated area (near Ste. Mere Eglise) slipping past under the belly of the ship; I turned around and shouted to the men of the stick, who were hooked up and ready to go: "Don't forget, everybody: as you go out the door, be sure to holler, 'Bill Lee."

The fact that you feel that we have done well is a source of great pride and satisfaction to all of us, for we realize that you have forgotten more about parachute troops than we will ever learn if we live to be a hundred. And I know I express the feelings of every officer and enlisted man in this regiment when I say that we keenly felt your absence on "D" day, and wished more than everything that you could have been with us to lead us in the action which brought to fruition the years of labor that you gave in order that, on the appointed hour, the parachute troops would be ready.

The Division did a grand job; everyone knows it and admits it; and I do not have to describe to you the swagger with which the members of your Division walk the streets, proudly exhibiting their Eagles, and not yielding an inch to anyone!

Yours sincerely,

George V. H. Moseley, Jr.

HEADQUARTERS 101st AIRBORNE DIVISION

OFFICE OF THE COMMANDING GENERAL

APO 472, U. S. Army
16 March 1945

Major General W. C. Lee,
Box 471,
Dunn, North Carolina.

Dear Bill:

We are all back resting again after our tour of duty at Bastogne and in Alsace. I expect you know as much of Bastogne as I do. I got into town the 27th of December and found the Division in fine shape with suprisingly low casualties and raring to go. The battle for the town continued until about the 10th of January, when the units on our right and left finally came up alongside. The Division then joined the offensive which finally liquidated the Ardennes pocket.

The day after we were withdrawn into Corps reserve we were suddenly thrown into open trailers in the middle of a blizzard and rushed down into Alsace in the Seventh Army sector. I will never know what the rush was all about as we took over a quiet sector which provided little excitement. As a matter of fact, it was an excellent training ground for our replacements with just enough activity to break them in gradually.

As always, we seem to lose a large number of our key officers. Julian Ewell, commanding the 501st, was wounded at Bastogne but will eventually come back. Stopka, commanding Bob Cole's old battalion, was killed. Salee and Inman, battalion commanders in the 327th, were wounded and Salee is a permanent loss. Mike Michaelis had a recurrence of his Holland wound and gone back to the U. S. Ned Moore is the new Chief of Staff. As a matter of fact, when I count noses now I find that of the team that went into Normandy only one General Officer (myself), two General Staff Officers, one Regimental Commander and two Battalion Commanders now occupy their old jobs. The durable battalion commanders are Strayer and Allen.

Our losses didn't end when we left the front. We had a grenade throwing exhibition using a new type of grenade here last week in which a premature wounded eleven officers, including Jerry Higgins, lightly, and Harry Kinnard, badly. Harry has been a brilliant G-3 and will now be lost for a couple of months. I have called in Charlie Chase to pinch-hit with the idea of puting Ewell in that position when he returns. I am afraid the latter's foot injury may preclude his jumping and hence eliminate him as a parachute regimental commander.

Yesterday was a great day in the history of the Division, one which we would have all given much to have you attend. General Eisenhower, with much supporting brass, came out to camp and presented the Division with unit citation for Bastogne. We had the Division review for him and everything went off very well. From all the press coverage I hope that you will be able to read about it and possibly see it in the news films. The 101 will really have to watch its step from now on.

Bud and Gerry Chapman are about now looking very harassed. Matt is, as usual, in fine form. Jerry Higgins is his usual efficient self but enjoying his rations too much to the extent that I am going to have to put him on a diet. Tony McAuliffe's replacement is Bill Gillmore, a football star of the class of '25. He had been artillery commander of the 1st Armored Division and will make a very fine Airborne reinforcement.

Please drop me a note and tell me how you are doing and if there is any chance of your coming over. We will sure turn out the guard if you will come to see us.

With best wishes to Mrs. Lee I am,

Sincerely yours,

Max

HEADQUARTERS 101ST AIRBORNE DIVISION

OFFICE OF THE ASSISTANT DIVISION COMMANDER

Berchtesgaden, Germany,
17 May 1945.

Dear Bill:

As you can see from the heading, we are now at Hitler's Retreat - a beautiful place, to say the least. So grand in appearance that I must agree with one parachutist who looked it over and remarked: "That bird Hitler must have been crazy - to want any other country when he already had something like this!"

We are nicely set up here - in Keitel's old headquarters. It is so well laid out that we are afraid it is too good - other and higher commands have their eye on this place, and it looks like only a matter of time. We are making the most of it while we may however.

Your letter of March 30th mentions a possible trip over here. If they wouldn't let you go before, fearing we would be busy in combat, you have them on that now - we aren't doing a darn thing! So - see if you can't do some fast talking now - this is the place to do the job, and we are all looking forward to seeing you.

Not much in the way of recent operations. We moved from Mourmelon to Cologne, and spent about three weeks there in "watchful waiting" while the Ruhr was cleared up across the river. Then we moved out to Seventh Army - by rail, plane, boat, truck and anything else we could lay hands on! Spent about two weeks getting the Division assembled, and then got into action on the very tail end of the show.

Lt. Col. Ray Allen is in the same situation as Tommy Wilder - although it occurred differently. A crime - just a short time before it was over. Otherwise, all the old gang is coming along fine - getting a good rest, and of course anxious to get home. You probably know the answer to that one. We hope to get a fair number home on the point system. However, we have lost so many of our older men, and we get credit for only two campaigns (due to the timing); in addition we cannot count the Distinguished Unit Citation, so all in all not too many will be affected. We will probably lose some to Gerry's unit in the not too distant future, however.

Hope you are continuing those fishing expeditions. Tommy Wilder wrote us of the grand time he had on his visit, and he is evidently in fine spirits. Suppose it is really hot in North Carolina now - here we have snow and ice, and we need plenty of blankets at night!

All for now. My very best to Dava and all my friends in Dunn.

Sincerely,

Jerry

From: Lieutenant General F.A.M. Browning, CB, DSO.

HEADQUARTERS, SUPREME ALLIED COMMANDER,
SOUTH EAST ASIA.

23rd October, 1945.

Dear Bill

I was delighted to receive your letter of 9th July, and my only reason for not replying long ago is the incredible spate of problems we have had to compete with since the Japanese threw in their hand.

I am more than sorry that the doctors have turned you down, but I envy your occupation of gentleman farmer. In fact I have been canvassing a theory that all officers of my age in the British Army should be politely shelved forthwith, but so far with no success!

News of the Airborne Divisions still comes through to me occasionally. I hear that Matt Ridgway is now D.S.A.C. in the Mediterranean and Max Taylor installed at West Point. Quite evidently we brought them up on the right lines! My old 5th Parachute Brigade is now out here doing garrison duties at Singapore.

Since I last wrote to you the whole picture in South East Asia has, of course, changed completely. The military problem of beating the Japs out of Burma was simple compared with the intricacies of getting the French back into Indo-China and the Dutch into the Netherlands East Indies! After three months of competing with political and diplomatic nightmares, and the rehabilitation of Burma and Malaya I am still looking for the drill for it all.

With 1,500,000 square miles in our theatre, some 128,000,000 inhabitants, and 500,000 Japs to disarm, not to mention the 100,000 prisoners of war and internees we have released and shipped home, you can see that there is a fair amount to be done.

You may have read that I went to deal with the Japanese surrender envoys in Rangoon last August. They were not an impressive collection of individuals and when they arrived seemed not to have hoisted in the fact that they had been defeated. However, after working them over for some time they reached a state when they signed without even looking at the paper! Since then the Japs have, as elsewhere, been very amenable and have given very little trouble; apart, that is, from their inefficient administration, which has to be seen to be believed!

I am looking forward to another letter from you when you have the lieusure to write. Meanwhile I hope you are taking good care of yourself and not overdoing things.

Yours ever

Boy.

P.S. Please remember me to Mrs Lee

24
So Long, Bill
1948

2 THE NEWS AND OBSERVER, RALEIGH, N. C., MONDAY MORNING, JUNE 28, 1948.

LAST RITES HELD FOR GENERAL LEE

Thousands Attend Rites for Dunn Native Who Founded Airborne Tactics

Dunn, June 27.—One of the greatest throngs of people ever to attend a funeral or any other occasion in this town gathered today to pay final tribute to Major General William C. Lee, the town's most famous citizen and father of America's airborne troops.

After a simple Episcopalian ceremony and a final military salute by the Army, the 53-year-old general—the man who showed the rest of the world how effectively to use airborne troops in warfare—was buried in Greenwood Cemetery. Thousands of people lined the big cemetery and others were parked in cars many blocks away in every direction, unable to get near the scene as more than 600 troops stood at attention as an honor guard and heard the rifle squad fire the traditional three volleys accorded military men.

Among the troops were hundreds of GIs who served under the famous general in Europe. Also present were some of the nation's top airborne generals and heroes of some of the most famous battles of the war. They had participated in the mighty airborne assault on Europe which General Lee had mapped and planned for months. It was General Lee who personally wrote the airborne doctrine and tactical procedures used in the D-Day invasion of the continent.

Among those who attended the services were Major General Anthony C. McAllifee, his former assistant commander and hero of Bastogne, Major General James (Slim Jim) Gavin, famed former commander of the 82nd Airborne Division and now chief of staff of the Fifth Army in Chicago and Major General Maxwell D. Taylor former 101st commander and now superintendent of the Military Academy at West Point. All of them were associates of General Lee and most of them had served under him as young lieutenants.

Forced into retirement by a heart ailment that prevented him from participating in the invasion, General Lee watched "my boys," as he called them, rise to worldwide fame in combat.

An honor guard of overseas veterans stood watch over the casket all yesterday and through the night.

United States Senator-nominate J. M. Broughton, with Mrs. Broughton, headed scores of State officials and dignitaries present for the funeral. Practically all State college and governmental departments were represented. Riding up front near the head of the procession was 80-year-old Dr. W. R. Cullom, retired head of the Bible department at Wake Forest College.

The funeral rites were read in the ... home of the general by the Rev. William Latta, rector of St. Stephens Church at Erwin and Bishop Edwin Penick of Raleigh. General Lee was a member of St. Stephens Church. The funeral procession left the home and moved westward to Orange Avenue then south to Greenwood Cemetery. The marching troops joined the procession at Pope Street. They were commanded by Lt. Colonel F. S. Holcome of the 82nd Airborne Division. The troops comprised the second battalion of the 504 airborne infantry. Major General C. E. Byers, commanding general of the 82nd, was the War Department's official representative although Secretary of the Army Kenneth Royall had sent a message in which he declared, "with the passing of General Lee our country has lost a truly magnificent soldier whose record of achievement and devotion to the service marked him as one of the outstanding sons of North Carolina and of the Army."

Another tribute was received from Lt. General F. A. M. Browning, chief of Great Britain's airborne forces, a second cousin of the King and an aide of Princess Elizabeth who worked closely with General Lee in Europe.

"On behalf of all British airborne forces who served with Bill Lee," said his cable, "I send you sincerest and deepest sympathy in your loss. Bill was greatly loved and respected by us all. For myself I mourn the loss of a dear personal friend."

Surrounding all the dignitaries at the funeral today were hundreds of General Lee's fellow townsmen. Rotarians, Legionnaires, reserves and National Guardsmen were all present for the rites. Serving as personal aides to Mrs. Lee were Lt. Colonel W. F. Stewart, an air force pilot who served as General Lee's air officer overseas and Captain William D. Cann.

Among the distinguished Army personnel here were Major General S. I. Irvin, commander of Ft. Bragg; Brig. Gen. C. D. W. Canham, assistant commander of the 82nd; Colonel Robert Sink, commandant of troops at West Point; Colonel Thomas Sherbourne of West Pint; Colonel Joseph H. Harper Bilder, infantry commander of the armed forces staff college; Colonel Pinky Ginder, Colonel J. P. Lake of Walter Reed Hospital in Washington, and many others.

Among the floral tributes was a reproduction of the 82nd's insignia, sent by the men of that outfit, in which more than 1,000 red roses and carnations were used to create the design.

Bill was buried on June 27, 1948 in a ceremony attended by thousands of people including more than 600 military troops and numerous distinguished Army personnel.

"With the passing of General Lee our country has lost a truly magnificent soldier whose record of achievement and devotion to the service marked him as one of the outstanding sons of North Carolina and of the Army."

Kenneth Royall
Secretary of the Army

"On behalf of all British airborne forces who served with Bill Lee, I send you sincerest and deepest sympathy in your loss. Bill was greatly loved and respected by us all. For myself I mourn the loss of a dear personal friend."

Lt. General F.A.M. Browning
Chief of Great Britain's airborne forces

Many of the now famous Lee men came to pay their tributes. Notable among them are Maxwell Taylor, Tony McAuliffe, and Jim Gavin.

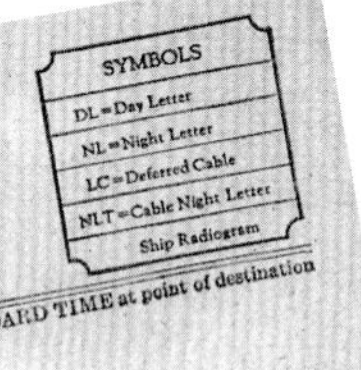

WESTERN UNION

JOSEPH L. EGAN, PRESIDENT

CLASS OF SERVICE: This is a full-rate Telegram or Cablegram unless its deferred character is indicated by a suitable symbol above or preceding the address.

SYMBOLS: DL = Day Letter; NL = Night Letter; LC = Deferred Cable; NLT = Cable Night Letter; Ship Radiogram

RGD99 PD=ELMCITH NCAR JUN 26 245P=
=MRS DAVA JOHNSON LEE=BD=

=GENERAL LEE WAS MY INSTRUCTOR AT STATE IN TWENTY THREE AND FOUR. HE HAS ALWAYS BEEN MY IDEAL SOLDIER, OFFICER, AND GENTLEMAN MY DEEPEST SYMPATHY TO YOU AND FAMILY=

=THEODORE B WINSTEAD MAJOR SIGNAL CORPS=

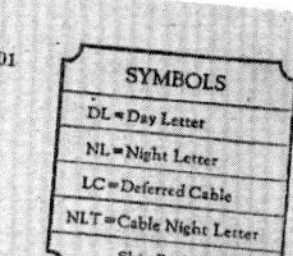

WESTERN UNION

JOSEPH L. EGAN, PRESIDENT

CLASS OF SERVICE: This is a full-rate Telegram or Cablegram unless its deferred character is indicated by a suitable symbol above or preceding the address.

SYMBOLS: DL = Day Letter; NL = Night Letter; LC = Deferred Cable; NLT = Cable Night Letter; Ship Radiogram

The filing time shown in the date line on telegrams and day letters is STANDARD TIME at point of origin. Time of receipt is STANDARD TIME at point of destination

.RGD76 PD=TDGL OYSTERBAY NY JUN 26 1111A
=MRS WILLIAM CLEE=BD=

=ON BEHALF ALL BRITISH AIRBORNE FORCES WHO SERVED WITH BILL LEE I SEND YOU SINCEREST AND DEEPEST SYMPATHY IN YOUR LOSS BILL WAS GREATLY LOVED AND RESPECTED BY US ALL FOR MYSELF I MOURN THE LOSS OF A DEAR PERSONAL FRIEND=

=BOY BROWNING=

=BOY..

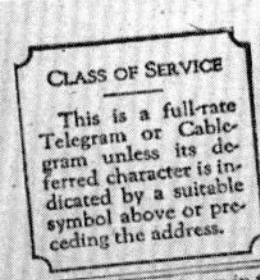
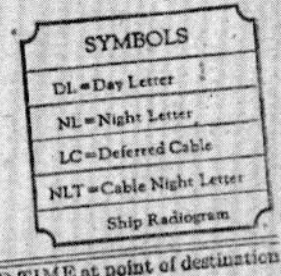

WESTERN UNION

JOSEPH L. EGAN, PRESIDENT

CLASS OF SERVICE: This is a full-rate Telegram or Cablegram unless its deferred character is indicated by a suitable symbol above or preceding the address.

SYMBOLS: DL = Day Letter; NL = Night Letter; LC = Deferred Cable; NLT = Cable Night Letter; Ship Radiogram

The filing time shown in the date line on telegrams and day letters is STANDARD TIME at point of origin. Time of receipt is STANDARD TIME at point of destination

.RGD82 DL GOVT PD=FZ FTBRAGG NCAR JUN 26 1152A
=MGS WILLIAM C LEE=BD=

REGRET DEEPLY TO LEARN OF THE DEATH OF GENERAL LEE PD PLEASE PERMIT ME TO EXTEND TO YOU MY PERSONAL SYMPATHY FOR YOUR GREAT LOSS PD WITH THE PASSING OF GENERAL LEE OUR COUNTRY HAS LOST A TRULY MAGNIFICIENT SOLDIER WHOSE RECORD OF ACHEIVEMENT AND DEVOTION TO THE SERVICE MARKED HIM AS ONE OF THE OUTSTANDING SONS OF NORTH CAROLINA AND OF THE ARMY=

=KENNETH C ROYALL SECRETARY OF THE ARMY WASHINGTON DC=

=PD PD

THE COMPANY WILL APPRECIATE SUGGESTIONS FROM ITS PATRONS CONCERNING ITS SERVICE

CLASS OF SERVICE
This is a full-rate Telegram or Cablegram unless its deferred character is indicated by a suitable symbol above or preceding the address.

WESTERN UNION

JOSEPH L. EGAN
PRESIDENT

1201

SYMBOLS
DL=Day Letter
NL=Night Letter
LC=Deferred Cable
NLT=Cable Night Letter
Ship Radiogram

The filing time shown in the date line on telegrams and day letters is STANDARD TIME at point of origin. Time of receipt is STANDARD TIME at point of destination

.RGD96 PD=WEST POINT NY JUN 25 230P

=MRS W C LEE=BD:

=DEEPLY MOVED BY NEWS OF BILLS DEATH YOU HAVE ALL OUR SYMPATHY=

MAX AND DIDDY TAYLOR:

=DIDDY:

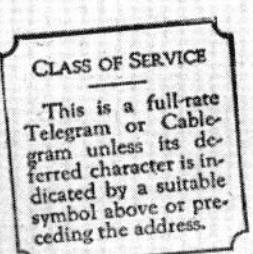
CLASS OF SERVICE
This is a full-rate Telegram or Cablegram unless its deferred character is indicated by a suitable symbol above or preceding the address.

WESTERN UNION

JOSEPH L. EGAN
PRESIDENT

1201

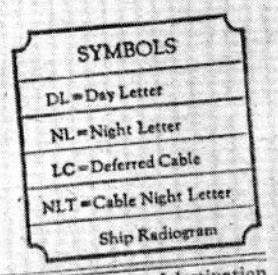
SYMBOLS
DL=Day Letter
NL=Night Letter
LC=Deferred Cable
NLT=Cable Night Letter
Ship Radiogram

The filing time shown in the date line on telegrams and day letters is STANDARD TIME at point of origin. Time of receipt is STANDARD TIME at point of destination

,RGD89 DL GOVT PD=FZ FTBRAGG NCAR JUN 26 135P=

MRS WILLIAM C LEE=BD=

:IT WAS WITH A FEELING OF PERSONAL LOSS THAT I LEARNED OF THE DEATH OF YOUR HUSBAND AND I EXTEND MY DEEPEST SYMPATHY TO YOU IN YOUR BEREAVEMENT=

:OMAR N BRADLEY OFFICE CHIEF OF STAFF US ARMY WASHINGTON DC=

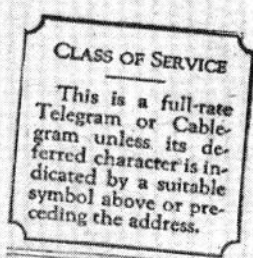
CLASS OF SERVICE
This is a full-rate Telegram or Cablegram unless its deferred character is indicated by a suitable symbol above or preceding the address.

WESTERN UNION

JOSEPH L. EGAN
PRESIDENT

1201

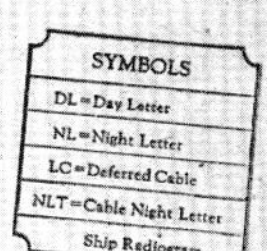
SYMBOLS
DL=Day Letter
NL=Night Letter
LC=Deferred Cable
NLT=Cable Night Letter
Ship Radiogram

The filing time shown in the date line on telegrams and day letters is STANDARD TIME at point of origin. Time of receipt is STANDARD TIME at point of destination

.RGD63 DL PD=RALEIGH NCAR JUN 26 1046A:

=MRS WILLIAM C LEE=BD

=I AM DEEPLY DISTRESSED TO LEARN OF THE DEATH OF YOUR BELOVED HUSBAND WHOSE WARM PERSONAL FRIENDSHIP I HAVE CHERISHED FOR MANY YEARSHE WAS INORTH CAROLINA'S MOST DISTINGUISHED SOLDIER AND HIS REMARKABLE CAREER HAS GIVEN HIM A LARGE PLACE THE ESTEEM OF OUR PEOPLE. HIS DEATH IS A GREAT LOSS TO THE AND NATION. MRS. BROUGHTON AND I PLAN TO ATTEND THE AND WE EXTEND TO YOU AND MEMBERS OF THE FAMILY OUR SYMPATHY IN YOUR GREAT LOSS.

OMPANY WILL APPRECIATE SUGGESTIONS FROM ITS

J MELVILLE BROUGHTON=

DAVA JOHNSON LEE
FEBRUARY 22, 1895
MARCH 2, 1983

Dava Johnson Lee stands in front of the General Lee historical marker at the corner of West Broad Street and South King Avenue. The marker was erected in September of 1949. In the background is the main street of Dunn. The building closest to the marker, unseen, is the First Baptist Church.

25
Honors

Would General Lee be pleased with all these honors? Answering in the affirmative requires some hesitation. Every single time he was honored, he tried in some way try to discount the honor—not saying that he wasn't important, but always pointing out how others contributed. A typical comment made by the general went something like this, "So often, when my loyal friends exaggerate my modest accomplishments, I have the uncomfortable feeling of being a fraud. I don't know who dubbed me the 'Father of the Airborne,' but in reality that term is a misnomer. I was only one of a number of men who contributed to the initial airborne effort."

He would usually go on to say something like, "But since I am one of those who have been intimately associated with the project from the beginning, naturally, I am tremendously proud of the magnificent achievements of our airborne troops on the battlefields throughout the world. So, it is on their behalf that I acknowledge this honor."

More than one newspaper account has said something like this:"To the people of his hometown, he's just plain Bill Lee—a soldier, a farmer, a good baseball player in the old days, a hometown boy who made good. He was the last man in the world who would claim credit for anything. When something was accomplished in his outfit, he gave the men credit and shied clear of any glory himself. Asked on a radio program once who was the most important man in the Army, the General replied without hesitation, 'the buck private, of course.' That was Bill Lee's nature all up and down. One of the things that bothered him most was publicity about himself. 'Write about the men and for goodness sakes, leave Bill Lee's name out of it,' he once told a reporter. There was nothing he enjoyed more than spending a day looking over his farm or visiting with friends. He called the old-timers by their first names and liked to recall the days when he played baseball on the sandlots around Dunn."

This is who General William Carey Lee is. He is the Father of the Airborne, and he is also just plain Bill. Let it suffice to say that we honor General Lee for ourselves—we need to insure that he takes his proper place in the history of our country.

Citation for the Distinguished Service Medal

Major General William C. Lee, United States Army. For exceptionally meritorious and distinguished service rendered in a duty of great responsibility while organizing and establishing the Airborne Command, Fort Bragg, North Carolina for the training of airborne units. Through his creative genius he inaugurated and supervised the training of the original parachute groups in the Army of the United States from which the airborne units were developed.

As the result of his efforts the airborne program which exists at the present time was instituted. Major General Lee was instrumental in the establishment of the Parachute School, Fort Benning, Georgia, 15 May 1942. With meager facilities, a few partially trained instructors, and by exceptional ability, force of character and the will to get the job done he built the framework for a powerful striking force.

The creation of the Airborne Command was the first effort of the United States to train airborne units on a major scale.

Medal awarded February 26 by Major General Rinehart at 302 General Hospital.

Buildings and Streets Commemorate General Lee

ABOVE: The Lee Field House, at Fort Bragg, North Carolina. This building has enabled many a paratrooper to stay in top physical condition.

BELOW: A street at Camp Chickamauga, Beppu, Japan is named in honor of General Lee.

Lee Village, at Fort Campbell, Kentucky is a family housing area named for the General.

NORTH CAROLINA STATE
OF THE UNIVERSITY OF NORTH CAROLINA
AT RALEIGH

OFFICE OF THE CHANCELLOR

16 July 1964

Mrs. William Carey Lee
209 West Divine Street
Dunn, North Carolina

Dear Mrs. Lee:

You will be interested in recent action of the Board of Trustees of the University of North Carolina which approved our recommendation to name our newest dormitory in honor of your late husband, Major General William Carey Lee. I am especially pleased to let you know this, and at some future date we will be in touch with you again when arrangements have been made for formal dedicatory ceremonies for which we would want you, your family and friends present.

We feel very honored that our new, magnificent building to house men students will carry the name, Lee Dormitory.

Sincerely,

John T. Caldwell

THE JOURNAL, NOVEMBER 1976

Statue Honors William Lee

Lee Residence Hall now has a statue to join it in honoring the man whose name it bears—Major General William C. Lee, father of the American airborne.

He was a native of Dunn and attended N.C. State during World War I. Later he returned to State and taught military science here from 1922 to 1926.

The statue was unveiled June 6 in Dunn. The citizens there had a special fund-raising effort to finance it.

Chancellor John W. Harrelson and UNC President Frank Porter Graham joined in presenting Lee an honorary doctor of military science degree in 1945 following World War II. In that war the 101st Airborne Division, which Lee organized, was a major element in the American forces liberating Europe.

In 1965, NCSU dedicated what then was the largest university dormitory in the state to Lee. Built at a cost of $2.5 million, it houses 840 students.

Chancellor John T. Caldwell and President William C. Friday joined Mrs. Lee and others in the dedication ceremonies.

Lee's portrait is prominently displayed in the dormitory.

OPPOSITE:
Mrs. Lee looks at the statue of General Lee originally in front of the Town Hall and later moved to the Museum at 209 West Divine Street.

WILLIAM C. LEE

Dunn, Best Town Under the Sun

Someone has said that between Virginia pretentiousness and South Carolina haughtiness lies a vale of humility called North Carolina. I think so. During this project, my feelings have been terribly reinforced as I've shared so many of General Lee's emotions about our hometown.

I don't know who coined the phrase, "Dunn, Best Town under the Sun," but from my perspective, it's true. I remember so many unique experiences that attest to the specialness of the town. One Saturday morning, I was sitting outside the old Dunn Theater waiting for it to open, and one of my teachers spied me reading a comic book. She grabbed me by the arm, marched me across the street and made me get a library card. When I was in fifth grade, my brother Corb was working at the old J and W Grocery and Ms. Owens told him I was not doing my homework. I shaped up.

As teenagers standing on the corner outside of Butler and Carroll's drugs, it was a regular exercise to ogle the passersby, but only until one of the town fathers would tell us to get home and go to work. We did. Sports were always part of life growing up and our coaches—Paul Waggoner, Troy Godwin and later Jim Brown and Whit Bradham—were powerfully special role models. They watched over their charges with an eye to life rather than sports.

Dunn, North Carolina, was linked inextricably to the military by General Lee and now the town, through the General Lee Airborne Museum, has made it a forever connection. It is a bridge to the past but also to the future. And, for our town, the future is bright, The General would definitely be pleased.

The General William C. Lee Airborne Museum began in the heart and mind of Hoover Adams, the publisher and founder of the Dunn, North Carolina *Daily Record.* In 1943 and 1944, then-Lieutenant Adams was General Lee's right-hand man, most notably during that period when the 101st Airborne began training in Europe for the D-Day invasion. It isn't my intent to give credit to one person or even those early pioneers with the vision for the Lee Museum, but to say thanks and give recognition of their great efforts.

The individuals themselves, if left to their own choices, would prefer to remain anonymous in the spirit of General Lee himself.

More than anything else, this tenth year commemoration of the General William C. Lee Airborne Museum is testimony to the dedication and commitment of an entire community. The museum is located at 209 West Divine Street, Dunn, North Carolina and is staffed by a wonderfully dedicated team, Tammy Williams, Janet Maynard, Sue Johnson, Eunice Moore and Eugene Williams. Their desire is, in the words of retired Air Force Colonel Ray Whitaker, "When people say General Lee, we want them to mean William C., not Robert E."

TO GET THERE: From Fayetteville, North Carolina or the Fort Bragg area, travel Interstate 95 North to exit 73 (Campbell University Exit); then 421 North (Cumberland Street) to South King Avenue and turn left; continue one block. The General Lee Airborne Museum is straight ahead on the corner of South King Avenue and West Divine Street.

Museum hours are Monday-Friday, 10-4; and Saturday, 11-4; Sunday, 1-4; closed Thanksgiving and Christmas days. Group tours are available during and after regular hours by appointment. Phone, 910-892-1947.

Selected Bibliography

Birdsong, George P. Jr.: *Stormy Weather*, Hambleden Publishing Co., Pleasanton, CA , 1991.

Bradley, General Omar N.: *A Soldier's Story*, Henry Holt, New York, 1951.

Brinkley, David: *Washington Goes To War*, Ballantine Books, New York, 1988.

Carter, Ross S.: *Those Devils in Baggy Pants*, Appleton-Century-Crofts, New York, 1951.

Casdorph, Paul D.: *Let The Good Times Roll, Life at Home in America During WW II*, Paragon House, New York, 1989.

Coultass, Clive: *Images for Battle*, Associated University Presses, Cranbury, NJ, 1989.

Department of the Army Pamphlet 20-260: *The German Campaign in the Balkans*, Dept. of Army, Washington, DC, 1963.

Gavin, Lt. Gen. James M.: *Airborne Warfare*, Infantry Journal Press, Washington, DC, 1947.

Green, Herman P.: *A History of Dunn N. C.*, Twyford Printing Co., Dunn, NC, 1985.

Koskimaki, George E.: *D-Day with The Screaming Eagles*. House of Print, Madelia, MN,1970.

Leckie, Robert: *The Wars of America*, Harper and Row, New York, 1968.

Lee, William C.: "Air Infantry," *Infantry Journal*, Vol. 58, No. 1 (1941), pp. 14-21.

___________: "The Use of Inherent Mobility," *Infantry Journal*, Vol. 43, No.1 (1936), pp. 10-12.

Lemmon, Sarah McCulloh: *North Carolina's Role in World War II*, State Department of Archives and History, Raleigh, NC, 1964.

Marshal, Gen. S. L. A.: *Night Drop*. Little, Brown and Company, Boston, 1962.

Mraza, Col. James E.: *The Glider War*, St. Martin's Press,New York, 1975.

North Carolina State College of Agriculture and Engineering College Catalog, 1922-1923 , p. 12.

Raff, Edson D.: *We Jumped to Fight*, Eagle, New York, 1944.

Rapport, Leonard, and Northwood, Arthur, Jr.: *Rendezvous with Destiny: A History of the 101st Airborne Division*, Infantry Journal Press, Washington, DC, 1948.

Reagan, Alice Elizabeth: *North Carolina State University: A Narrative History*, North Carolina State University Foundation and the North Carolina State Alumni Association, 1987.

_____________: *A Bridge Too Far*, Simon and Schuster, New York, 1974.

Ryan, Cornelius: *The Longest Day*, Simon and Schuster, Inc., New York, 1959

Taylor, Maxwell D.: *Swords and Plowshares*, W. W. Norton and Co., Inc., New York: , 1972.

The Agromeck (North Carolina State College Yearbook), 1917, pp. 152-153.

The Heritage of Harnett County North Carolina, Volume 1, 1993.

The News and Observer: "Last Rites for General lee," June 28, 1948.

Recommended Reading

The following books are my personal favorites with comments. In reading them, I was continually struck with the wonderful fraternity of paratroopers. It was as though the authors were entrusted with a sacred mission; almost burdened with the task of recording their odysseys with great accuracy. I know I feel it.

Allen, Patrick H. F.: *Screaming Eagles*. Mallard Press, New York, 1990. (Only a small section on the history of the 101st, but very well done with some good photos.)

Bando, Mark A., *The 101st Airborne at Normandy*. Motorbooks International, Osceola, WI, 1994. (Very inspiring and original; much material from soldiers' personal accounts and photographs. The author is incredibly candid in his descriptions.)

Blair, Clay: *Ridgway's Paratroopers*. The Dial Press, New York, 1985. (Written from a definite perspective reinforcing the idea that events are often colored based on who is telling the story.)

Booth, Michael T. and Spencer, Duncan: *Paratrooper*. Simon and Schuster, New York, 1994. (Wonderfully honest account of one of General Lee's boys. Gavin was one of the truly heroic figures of World War II.)

Breuer, William B.: *Geronimo!: American Paratroopers in World War II*. St. Martin's Press, New York, 1989. (*Geronimo* is actually dedicated to General Lee. A terrific book, extremely readable and based on interviews and diary entries of those who lived it; well written and researched.)

Devlin, Gerard M.: *Paratrooper*, St. Martin's Press, New York, 1979. (The bible of the development of the parachute; very objective).

Gabel, Kurt: *The Making of a Paratrooper*, University Press of Kansas, Lawrence, KS, 1990. (A personal favorite. Most valuable in understanding paratrooper training, plus descriptions of training areas.)

Hastings, Max: *Overlord, D-Day and the Battle for Normandy*, Simon and Schuster, New York, 1984. (Great description of the planning and execution of the cross-channel invasion. Very readable.)

Huston, James A.: *Out of the Blue*, Purdue University Studies, West Lafayette, Indiana, 1972. (Very scholarly book with treatment of subjects not often seen with detail and prominence. Extremely well documented.)

Mrozek, Steven J.: *Prop Blast, Chronicle of the 504th Parachute Infantry Regiment*. 82nd Airborne Division Historical Society, Fort Bragg, NC, 1986. (Delightful in its absolute originality. For the nonmilitary it would be good introduction to the actual thinking of a military airborne unit.)

Stallings, Laurence: *The Doughboys: The story of the AEF, 1917-1918*, Harper and Row, New York, 1963. (General Lee often referred to this book and kept it in his personal library. Good description of the training ideas of Black Jack Pershing.)